UTE MOUNTAIN TRIBAL PARK

(The Other Mesa Verde)

A Guide and Tribute
by Jean Akens

LION HOUSE

Copyright 1987
by Jean Akens

Published by
Four Corners Publications
P.O. Box 548
Moab, Utah 84532

Front Cover:
EAGLE'S NEST
   One of the most exquisite cliff dwellings in the Southwest. Perched like the nest of an eagle high above the depths of Lion Canyon, this village is visited on the Main Ruins tour.

ACKNOWLEDGEMENTS

The author wishes to acknowledge several individuals who helped with this book. First and foremost, my thanks go to Arthur Cuthair and his staff at Ute Mountain Tribal Park. Arthur's cooperation and cheerful assistance were invaluable, and the friendship of all of those who work so hard to make the dream of the park a reality is highly regarded. Thanks are also due to my husband, Jack Akens, and son, John Akens, for providing many of the pictures, and to my other son, Jeff Akens, for drawing the illustrations. Ber Knight of Moab, Utah served as editor and gave many helpful suggestions. F.A. Barnes, another resident of Moab, also deserves a big thank you for helping me to get "computerized" and thus get this book in print.

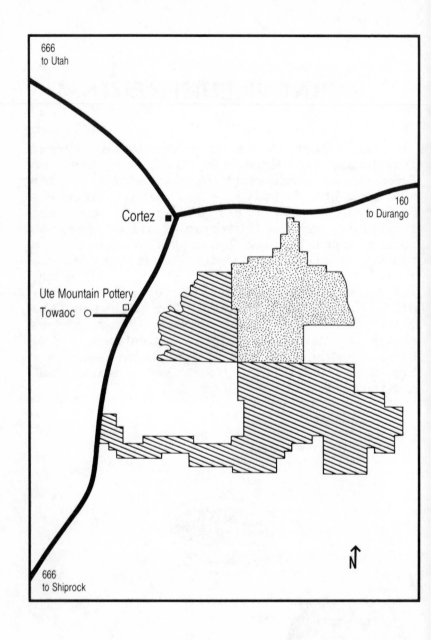

666
to Utah

160
to Durango

Cortez ■

Ute Mountain Pottery
Towaoc ○——— □

666
to Shiprock

N↑

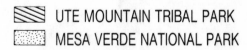

UTE MOUNTAIN TRIBAL PARK
MESA VERDE NATIONAL PARK

TABLE OF CONTENTS

INTRODUCTION

Tucked away in the southwest corner of Colorado is a park different from others, for it is a place to be experienced, not merely visited. It is not a park for the casual tourist, who expects to step from his air-conditioned auto or tour bus, take in the sights at a glance, snap a few pictures, then depart for the next stop on his itinerary. First, to visit Ute Mountain Tribal Park takes some prior consideration, some advance planning. Then, it requires a certain type of individual, a person who takes pleasure in the unusual, the sometimes physically challenging. A vivid imagination is helpful, and a sense for adventure, but foremost it takes someone prepared to take a step back in time--to the time of the Ancient Ones, those called the ANASAZI.

Ute Mountain Tribal Park is part of the Ute Mountain Ute Reservation. Encompassing 125,000 acres of sheer sandstone cliffs, green flat-topped plateaus, and deep rugged canyons, the park also includes a twenty-five mile stretch of the Mancos River, the waterway that cuts completely through the Mesa Verde.

Within the boundaries of the Ute Tribal Park are hundreds of known Anasazi surface ruins and cliff dwellings. Many of these are in their natural unexcavated state, which lends them a special charm. Others have been cleaned and stabilized for visitation but they, too, are out of the ordinary. Nowhere in the park is the sterile appearance usually associated with ruins in many archaeological parks.

Although an approved Ute guide must be in attendance in order to gain access to the area, once inside ruins, visitors are welcome to wander through many of the rooms, and encouraged to handle and photograph pottery sherds, corn grinding stones, remnants of tools and cordage, or other relics left behind by those who abandoned their homes some seven centuries past. To touch an artifact fashioned by the Anasazi so long ago somehow connects the modern visitor with the far distant past, and with the ones who chose to inhabit this stark but beautiful land.

Whether you prefer to take the standard Main Ruins tour or to arrange one that takes you to a more remote, seldom-visited area, at Ute Mountain Tribal Park you experience what it was like to live as did those ancient peoples. It is not unusual to come away feeling a certain oneness with those who are gone. Definitely, it is a visit you are not likely to forget.

TREE HOUSE

3

QUICK FACTS

LOCATION:

Ute Mountain Tribal Park is situated south and east of Cortez, Colorado, within the boundaries of the Ute Mountain Ute Reservation. More than twice the size of Mesa Verde National Park, Ute Mountain Tribal Park includes much of the western and southern sections of that great mesa. The forested uplands are cut by more than a dozen canyons that comprise the Mancos River drainage system. It is an area of scenic vistas, displaying nature at its rugged best, and is rich in archaeological treasures.

TOURS:

All tours are by advance reservation only. It is sometimes possible, however, to make arrangements on fairly short notice (a day or two) provided a guide or space on a tour is available. REMEMBER: No tours of the area may be made without an approved Ute guide in attendance. This is the homeland of the Anasazi and Ute. Respect it as such.

The standard tour to the Main Ruins area is a day-long visit which begins with a drive up the Mancos River Canyon, stopping at several points of interest. Next you are taken to the mesa top south of the river to a view point across the canyon from the ruins to be visited. The tour finishes with a mildly strenuous, approximately one mile, two hour hike down into the Lion Canyon arm of Johnson Canyon, where four sizable Anasazi cliff dwellings are visited. CAUTION: There are several ladders which must be negotiated in order to reach the ruins level. Also, there are no guard rails anywhere in the park. These factors should not present a problem if reasonable care is taken.

Tours begin at the Ute Mountain Pottery Factory twelve miles south of Cortez on U.S. Highway 666. Your guide will meet you there at 9:00 a.m. Arrive early enough to allow time to visit the pottery plant. The modern building houses a thriving business in the making of contemporary Indian pottery. The market for Ute ware has expanded rapidly in recent years, due to continual improvement in artistic quality.

You must provide your own lunch and transportation for the day. Have sufficient gasoline in your vehicle; the Main Ruins are approximately forty miles off the highway. Much of the road has been graveled and work proceeds on the remainder. Most passenger cars will have little difficulty with the roads, but dust can be a problem along the route. Rest assured, your destination is worth a little discomfort. Its remoteness is part of the charm.

ADDITIONAL TOURS:
There are endless opportunities for optional touring and exploration within the vast park (mostly on foot, hiking or backpacking) PROVIDED YOU ARRANGE FOR A GUIDE. Day hikes can be taken almost anywhere. Backpacking trips, usually lasting from overnight to a week, take you into remote areas and to seldom visited ruins. These are a special treat and one of the reasons the park is unique. Any of the optional tours will be tailored to your particular interest, but you must provide your own equipment and food.

CAMPING:
A small but delightful primitive campground, with shady, secluded sites, has been developed by the Utes beside the Mancos River, deep within the

canyon. For those who wish to stay overnight or longer, arrangements must be made with the Tribal Park office, and a permit obtained. Lodgings and complete hookup campgrounds are available in nearby Cortez.

SODA CANYON
This is typical of the many rugged chasms that form the drainage system of the Mesa Verde-- and make hiking the area an adventure.

SEASON:
The tour season generally runs from late spring through early fall. Groups or individuals may arrange for tours at other times of the year, weather permitting. A word of caution is also necessary here. During summer it can get quite hot, so come prepared with hat, sun lotion, and ALWAYS carry water. A rain jacket might come in handy in mid- to late-summer. Moreover, insects can be a problem early in the season, especially along the river, so bring repellent. Long pants

and a long sleeved shirt help reduce insect annoyance.

FEES:

The cost of the Main Ruins tour is $7.00 per person. For any group above twelve in number, the price is reduced to $6.00. Backpackers pay a $25.00 deposit per group and $20.00 per person, per day. These fees are subject to change, so it is best to verify beforehand. Also, any donations made to your guide or to the park are greatly appreciated. The Utes have little funds available to develop and maintain the park. Every dollar helps.

FURTHER INFORMATION:

For further information, to make reservations, or to request a free fact-filled color brochure, write to the park director:

Mr. Arthur Cuthair
Ute Mountain Tribal Park
Towaoc, CO 81334
or call: (303) 565-3751, ext. 282

FROM PAST TO PRESENT
A Brief Look at Ute and Tribal Park History

The Ute Mountain Utes presently reside in one of three reservations set aside by the United States Government for the Ute Indian people. Although U.S. citizens, they are considered a sovereign nation. Headquarters for the Tribal Council, the governing body for the reservations' some 1500 inhabitants, is located in the town of Towaoc, south of Cortez, Colorado. This population center lies in broad Montezuma Valley between sacred Sleeping Ute Mountain and the high escarpments of the Mesa Verde, a Spanish name meaning "Green Table."

Despite the familiar name "Yutas" applied to the tribe by the Spanish, the Utes refer to themselves as NUCHE, which translates to "we the people." Although a tribe never large in numbers, their domain once stretched from the eastern front range of the "Shining Mountains"--as the Rockies were called--westward into central Utah, and from the Green River in Wyoming south across Colorado into northern New Mexico. As early as the A.D. 1400's and quite possibly before, the Mancos Canyon and Mesa Verde area was part of their territory.

It is thought that the first Utes migrated into North America across the Bering Strait at a time when lower ocean levels exposed a dry land bridge. The dates of human migration have not been determined with certainty. The Utes themselves say they have been here from the beginning. In this belief, they may not be too far wrong. Many authorities now think that this tribe might be direct descendants of earlier Archaic groups, and possibly even the older Paleo-Indians, with residency in this country that extends as far back as ten to fifteen thousand years. Their language, called Uto-Aztecan, identifies them with the Shoshonean branch of Indians, along with the Paiute, Hopi, Comanche, Shoshone, Chemehuevi, and Bannock.

The early Utes led a somewhat difficult hunting and gathering type of existence. They were a society constantly on the move, as they followed game and ripening vegetation. Although primarily a mountain people who kept to themselves, the Utes often ventured onto the plains to hunt for game and foodstuffs--or enemies to raid. Fighting was a way of life for this independent warrior tribe and to die in battle was considered the ideal. Being one of the first North American tribes to acquire horses from the Spanish enabled the Utes to pursue their interests with the greater ease of mobility. They quickly became excellent horsemen, and the number of horses a man owned determined his wealth and quite often his social status.

Although in the distant past their numbers might have been different, in the 1800's there were three main tribes, with seven generally recognized bands, or sub-tribes, four in the north and three in the south. Each group had a carefully defined hunting territory, although winter and summer ranges were often in separate areas. While each individual Ute was affiliated with one of the aforementioned sub-tribes, most families chose to live or travel in smaller groups, banding together whenever necessary or desirable. Of the three Southern Ute bands, the Weeminuche was the largest. Ignacio, Weeminuche chief in the latter part of the nineteenth century--when the white man began to invade the country of the Ute in earnest--was leader over all

Southern Utes. His band occupied the San Juan River Valley and parts of northwestern New Mexico and southeastern Utah. It is the Weeminuche who now comprise most of the population of the Ute Mountain Ute Reservation.

CHIEF IGNACIO
Courtesy Colorado Historical Society - F42593
Weeminuche chief in the late 19th and early 20th centuries, Ignacio was responsible for the establishment of the Ute Mountain Ute Reservation.

Years of conflict with a series of outsiders, the Spanish, the fur trappers, the seekers after precious metals, and finally with the settlers, led to a campaign in the 1870's--headed by politicians and journalists in Denver--to rid Colorado of "the Ute menace." The scattered bands of Southern Utes, although far from the city, soon felt the effects of this pressure and began to seek areas unwanted by the white man in which to secrete themselves. One stronghold favored was the lower Mesa Verde and its many canyons. The ruins of the Ancient Ones, however, were left strictly alone. The Utes had no wish to anger the spirits in the burials associated with the ruins. To them, that was sacred and forbidden ground.

Although there were a few isolated episodes of violence throughout Colorado during this period, and rumors abounded concerning both real and supposed Indian atrocities, for the most part the Utes wanted nothing more than to be left alone. Under the leadership of Ouray, chief of the Tabeguche band of Northern Utes and the foremost spokesman and negotiator for all Utes, treaties had been signed which guaranteed them this right. But it was not to be, for the land of the Ute was much desired by the steadily increasing white population.

Ultimately, it was a relatively unimportant incident in the remote northwestern section of the territory that led to the end of a free life for all seven bands. It involved one Nathan Meeker and a small band of Northern Utes. Meeker had been sent from the east to serve as agent for the White River Indian Agency. The man was untrained and lacked knowledge of Indian culture, a combination doomed to fail.

Following the dictates of the Bureau of Indian Affairs, Meeker determined to make farmers out of once proud warriors, a change in lifestyle the Utes did not take kindly to. Stubbornness and lack of understanding led Meeker to make several costly mistakes in his dealings with the Utes, but violence did not erupt until the agent gave the order to plow up a large horse racing and pasture area that belonged to a medicine man. During a confrontation between Meeker and the Ute, Canalla by name, the White River agent was shoved against a wall, then pushed outside and knocked to the ground.

Nathan Meeker, instead of rationally assessing his situation and acknowledging his own responsibility for much of what had happened, hastily telegraphed a complaint to the governor and the Indian Bureau. An unfortunate chain of events was thus set in motion. Troops of cavalry, who had nothing better to do with the frontier wars by then all but over, were called out to quell the threat of "hostilities" at the White River Agency. But by marching onto Ute lands, the soldiers were violating the treaty arranged by Chief Ouray, and the agency Indians were understandably upset.

The White River Utes proceeded to band together with the intention of preventing the soldiers' advance with a display of numbers. Inadequately armed, they had no wish to engage the U.S. Cavalry in battle. However, when the two groups met, matters quickly got out of control. Among frightened horses and milling people with nerves on edge, it took but one unauthorized shot for a fight to commence. No one knows which side fired that fateful shot but the end result, after nearly a week of sporadic fighting, was the death of many Ute and Cavalrymen--and, at the White River Agency, the massacre of Meeker and six other government employees. Meeker's wife and daughter were abducted by the raiding party, along with another woman and her two daughters. The year was 1879.

When authorities with cool heads intervened and the complete story was pieced together, the furor soon diminished. Even the hostages were released unharmed after lengthy bargaining was concluded. But for the scattered Ute bands of Colorado and Utah, most of whom knew little or nothing about the Meeker Massacre, the damage was done. The white population was enraged, therefore the outcome was inevitable. In 1880 began the final banishment of the Utes to reservations, with the Southern Ute agency being formed in 1882.

For many years following, there remained problems for the Utes concerning reservation boundaries. It was not until the Hunter Act of 1895, that the question of territory was finally settled for the Southern Ute Bands. Other issues were also involved with the Act. Each Ute family had been offered private farms, usually a quarter section of land (160 acres). Although the Southern Utes were not as adverse to farming as were their northern relations, Chief Ignacio and the majority of his Weeminuche followers refused to accept individual family allotments, preferring to live on common ground owned by all--a practice still favored.

The 1895 legislation therefore provided this band with a separate tract of land in the extreme western portion of the Southern Ute Reservation, land which included Mesa Verde and the Mancos River Canyon. This Ute band, which had numbered 550 during an 1892 census, thereafter left the town named for their chief, Ignacio, Colorado, and headed toward the Four Corners. Some families chose to settle along the Mancos River where they could graze their livestock, while others built their shelters up on the surrounding mesa tops. More of them went on to Navajo Springs, where a sub-agency for the band was established. This headquarters was moved to Towaoc, about a mile north, in 1917.

There followed a long period of semi-isolation for the Weeminuche; assimilation into modern society was slow. Not until 1940, in fact, did they adopt their own constitution and set of written laws. Significant change began for them in the 1950's. Prior to that time, the Utes were still living in small groups all over the reservation. Then oil companies came to explore, some discoveries were made, and royalties were paid to the tribe, thus providing an unexpected source of income. Also, in 1959, a claim against the U.S. Government for Tribal lands never paid for was settled in the amount of thirty-two million dollars. This sum was divided among all the bands.

Since there was no longer a need to work the land for bare subsistence living, most everyone flocked to Towaoc to live in relative comfort. With the town burgeoning, the Weeminuche asked for an agency of the Bureau of Indian Affairs to be located there, separate from the Southern Ute Agency. Direct communication would then be possible. It was some time before their request became reality. Not until 1968 was the agency for the Ute Mountain Utes finally established.

Meanwhile, the money that had seemed such a blessing for the tribe began to run out. But by this time the Weeminuche had grown accustomed to town living and had no wish to return to the older, considerably more difficult, way of life. All too soon the tribe was going broke.

Fortunately, the Ute Mountain Utes had a chief with foresight. Chief Jack House had lived in the canyon of the Mancos in his younger days. He was familiar with the area and knew of its many Anasazi ruins. In 1967, when well along in his sixties, Chief Jack originated the idea for the Ute Tribal Park. It was his desire to preserve the ruins for the future, and to share them with

14

others. In doing so, some desperately needed
income would be generated for his people. His was
an idea opposed by many in the tribe, especially
those of his own generation. There still remained
a strong belief that no good could come from
disturbing the spirits of the Ancient Ones. But
the chief was not to be dissuaded. Proceeding
with his plans for the park, Jack House traveled
to Washington, D.C., where he succeeded in having
the status of Wilderness Area lifted from the
proposed park lands.

CHIEF JACK HOUSE
*Chief Jack House, whose Indian name meant
"Hand-in-the-Sun," originated the idea for the
Tribal Park.*

In the summer of 1971, crews began to clean and stabilize certain of the Lion Canyon cliff dwellings, preparing them for visitation. Archaeologists from the University of Colorado Mesa Verde Research Center worked in the area between 1972 and 1975, to record, preserve, and analyze the archaeological information of the ruins in the proposed Tribal Park, and to assist in the stabilization. One of the workers helping the scientists during those early years was a young Arthur Cuthair. He had done similar stabilization work at Mesa Verde National Park. His knowledge and experience led him to be offered the position of Ute Tribal Park Director, a post he has since filled with dedication and unbounded enthusiasm.

Chief Jack House died in August of 1971, during the first year of park preparation. He lived long enough, fortunately, to see his idea take shape and work on the project begun. Jack House was the last chief of the Ute Mountain Utes. An era, of untold ages, had come to an end. Now all governing is done by the Tribal Council, a group of elected officials.

Road work was needed to improve access into Mancos Canyon and the Lion-Johnson Canyon area. Archaeologists again returned to the reservation in 1976 to do salvage work on the road bed. This resulted in one final act of protest against the park, when Ute vandals burned down the abandoned home of Chief Jack House. Still the work went on, slowly, as funds became available. In 1981, a few tours were given, "sneak previews" of what was in store. The public reaction was favorable. The unusual type of tour experience offered by the Utes was well received and they were encouraged.

Progress continues for the entire tribe, as they face toward the future. Oil and gas rights again bring in some revenue. The Dolores River

Project has allocated water to the reservation, enough to irrigate 7,500 acres at the toe of Ute Mountain for agricultural use. The Weeminuche of the Ute Mountain Reservation now focus their time and energy inside their homeland, planning ahead. It is their goal to become self-sufficient, truly a nation unto themselves.

ARTHUR CUTHAIR
Taking a lunch break, Ute Mountain Tribal Park Director, Arthur Cuthair, sits on a narrow ledge in Inaccessible House. A man of dedication and strong belief in the future of the park, Cuthair has proved to be an excellent choice for the position of director.

DISTANT PAST
The Ancient Ones

Who were the first men to walk the Mancos River Canyon, to climb the steep cliffs to the green tableland above, to explore the many rugged canyons that carry run-off from the highlands to the river? No one knows. Nor can there be an accurate guess as to when this might have occurred. Perhaps Paleo-Indians, those who have been labeled Folsom or Clovis, passed through some ten to twenty thousand years ago, on the trail of game. Maybe they paused beside the river to quench their thirst, or spent a lonely night huddled around a campfire in the relative safety of some sheltered cliff alcove. If so, no evidence of their passing has been found.

It was not until around the year A.D. 1--give or take a few hundred years--that hunting and gathering bands of Native Americans grew tired of roaming the four-corners region and began to turn to the cultivation of crops for part of their food source. The primitive form of agriculture they practiced set the scene for a more sedentary way of life. A life from which a culture developed that would leave archaeological remains behind for future study, wonder, and speculation. No one knows by what name or names these people were called. The Navajo, themselves comparative newcomers to the Southwest, refer to them as the ANASAZI, the Ancient Ones.

Archaeologists have separated the Anasazi into different cultural time periods. The earliest are labeled the Basketmakers, due to a talent for the weaving of fine utilitarian baskets, as well as mats, sandals, belts, and an occasional pouch. Basketmakers lived near their fields during the planting and harvesting seasons in brush shelters or natural caves. Squash was cultivated, but corn--probably obtained originally from Mesoamerica--quickly became the mainstay of their diet. To supplement the family larder, the men hunted game with snares, spears, and the atlatl, or "throwing stick," a device which gives a short spear better range and accuracy. The women, when not tending children or gathering and preparing wild and cultivated foodstuffs, were most likely the ones who first learned the art of weaving. Their baskets were so tightly woven that, when lined with pitch, they were watertight. This enabled them to be used for cooking. Hot stones taken from the fire with stick tongs were dropped into a basket of stew or vegetables, and the action was repeated until the water boiled and the food was cooked. Undoubtedly, ashes coating the heated rocks also went into the meal, but this apparently did not concern the Basketmaker chef.

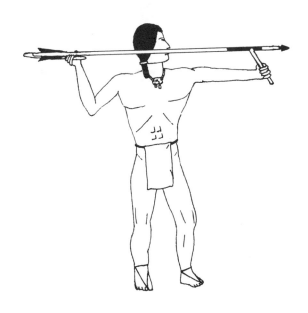

Another woven product in use during this time was hair cloth, the manufacture of which must have entailed much painstaking labor. The remains of most women of this period show them to have had short-cropped tresses, unlike the men who favored long, often elaborately dressed hair styles. Although several fine cloth pieces have been found made from dog hair, it is safe to assume that much of the hair for this unusual product came from the heads of the Anasazi females.

One other custom of Basketmaker women was the practice of weaving soft cradleboards of reeds and withes for their infants. To provide additional comfort, the women often cushioned the baby's head by placing a pillow between child and board. This cultural trait is important to remember, in light of a later change in cradleboard style.

Little clothing was worn by the Basketmakers--or by the Anasazi of any period. Attire for both male and female was limited to breechcloth or

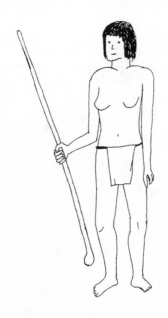

apron in warmer weather, with sandals woven from yucca fibers used to protect the feet. Large blankets that doubled as robes were woven from strips of fur wrapped around yucca-fiber cordage, and these as well as animal skins served as body coverings during the colder seasons. To decorate their person, the Ancient Ones made jewelry from stones, shells, bones, and seeds. Some of this material undoubtedly was obtained from far-ranging traders, for goods from the Mississippi River Valley and the Pacific Ocean found their way into Basketmaker homes. It was also during this time period that turquoise became popular. It, too, had to be acquired by trade or by the making of long journeys to the source, for none is found on or near the Mesa Verde.

By A.D. 550, change had occurred within the society of the Ancient Ones. Beans had been added to the list of cultivated crops and more varieties of maize had been developed. The bow and arrow had replaced the spear and atlatl, and crude pottery making had begun, the method for handling clay probably copied from neighbors to the south. Over the succeeding generations, the women learned to make bowls, pitchers, water jars, ladles, and cooking pots; archaeological excavations show gradual development in form, style, and the use and type of paint materials.

Known as the Modified Basketmaker Period because of the decline in the making of woven goods for culinary use, it was during this time that there is first undisputed evidence that the Anasazi had settled in the Mesa Verde area. Perhaps the Ancient Ones had determined that the region was favorable for farming, as it has a long frost-free growing season, the hot summer temperatures necessary for plant growth, and reasonably dependable mid- to late-summer rains. Conversely, winters usually do not have severe cold spells of any length, but do have sufficient

21

snowfall to thoroughly moisten the soil, an important factor when dry-farming is practiced.

To further attract the Anasazi to the locale, there was water from springs, pot holes or "tanks," and the river, as well as plenty of game. Natural foodstuffs such as yucca and cactus fruit, pine-nuts and acorns, and various berries and seeds were also readily available, and there was an abundant supply of wood for fuel, tool-making, and home construction. And it was in that latter category that perhaps the most significant cultural change occurred during the Modified Basketmaker Period. More permanent dwellings in the form of "pithouses" began to be built. Oblong holes were dug into the ground, ranging from one to several feet deep. These were lined with upright slabs of rock, sloping sides were raised, and finally the exterior was roofed over with brush and mud to form a plaster-like adobe coating.

The people of the Mesa Verde were still most likely few in number and lived in small family or clan groupings. With this complete change to a settled way of life, turkeys were domesticated and joined man's universal friend the dog as the only animals ever kept by the Anasazi. Other than as a food source, the bird's greatest contribution was its supply of feathers. The quills were split, then wrapped around yucca cordage and woven into heavy cloth. The dogs apparently served as pets or hunting companions; there is little evidence they were used for food.

Sometime around A.D. 700, the Ancient Ones started to congregate in larger numbers, and the construction of small, above-ground villages began. Called the Developmental Pueblo Period, the rooms built were generally rectangular, with vertical walls of post and adobe (jacal) in the beginning, and later of stone and mortar, most often plastered over. When joined end-to-end, these small sleeping and storage quarters often formed a long curving row. They were usually one-storied.

In front of the rooms were found one or more deep pithouses, which evolved throughout this period from storerooms into men's meeting and ceremonial chambers, known as "kivas." As the function of these rooms assumed religious significance, their shape also gradually changed from oblong to circular. While nearly all kivas have similar interior features--which are still found in contemporary Pueblo chambers--there are some variations seen throughout the area of occupation. This is especially true in certain kivas built later in cliff dwellings where alcove contour often dictated modifications.

Remember the soft cradleboard used by the Basketmakers? It was around this time that the practice of wrapping infants on hard boards, usually split planks, came into prominence. Considering the pliable infant skull, this often resulted in flattened, misshapen heads. Upon finding human remains of this type, archaeologists were at first confused. They assumed that a new race of people had come upon the scene, bringing the advanced architectural styles and other developments. In reality, cranial deformation probably began as a fad and grew in popularity until it became tradition, while the other cultural changes were merely the result of natural progression.

During the Developmental Pueblo Period, advances were made in every area except basketry, which declined as pottery making took precedence. The quality of workmanship in clay goods improved and corrugated pottery appeared which, when used as a cooking vessel, was better adapted to retain and distribute heat. Designs on non-cooking ware became more elaborate, with various styles and patterns rising and falling in popularity through the years. Much of the art work on these ancient pottery pieces is so beautiful that the making of clay goods must have been a source of pride for Pueblo Period women. For todays archaeologists, the study of pottery shapes and painted designs is a valuable method to date and classify ruins.

Around A.D. 900, cotton cloth appeared in the Mesa Verde area. The raw cotton was probably imported from warmer regions to the south where it could be cultivated, for there is no evidence that it was ever grown on or very near the mesa. The men, and possibly some of the women, became adept at weaving cloth, of which fine examples remain to this day. With the appearance of cotton, less hair cloth was needed and that practice then dwindled.

Late in the Developmental Pueblo Period came another significant architectural change, which continued through the next cultural period. The people began to build towers, many of them round in design, others square, rectangular, or D-shaped. Some were part of villages or were connected by tunnels to kivas; a few stood apart. Their exact purpose is uncertain--perhaps some were merely lookout posts--but there is speculation that they may have been used to observe the sun, and maybe the stars, to determine the correct time for planting or the scheduling of important ceremonies.

Pottery making and dwelling construction, along with various other art forms, reached peaks in the Mesa Verde region between A.D. 1100 and 1300, by which time the population numbered well into the thousands. Called the Great, or Classic Pueblo Period, it is so named because of the many well-built, often multi-storied, masonry structures that were erected. Stones used in the massive walls were carefully cut and neatly coursed. Most walls were smoothly plastered and sometimes decorated with brightly colored designs. However, it is in the plan of the Classic Pueblo village that is seen the greatest change. Kivas, once outside the town proper, were now placed inside. They were sunk deeper and surrounded by the living and storage rooms, their flat rooftops serving the populace as courtyards and work areas. And there were more of these ceremonial structures built than ever before.

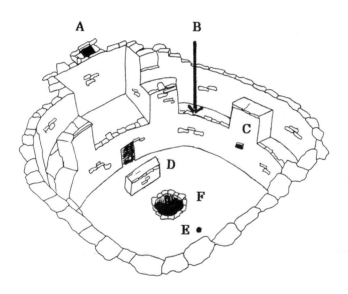

PARTS OF A KIVA

A. Ventilator shaft
B. Banquette (shelf)
C. Pilasters (to hold the roofing material)
D. Deflector
E. Sipapu (entrance to the underworld)
F. Firepit

Such cultural changes raise many questions. Was there a need for defense, for banding together in greater numbers? Had nomadic invaders begun to harass the Pueblo farmer, or did dissension among the Anasazi themselves cause the shift to larger, easier to defend population centers? Was the increase in the number of kivas an indication that the people felt the need to appease the gods for some reason? No one can say with any certainty. Perhaps the changes were merely the result of natural evolution in both lifestyle and religious customs. There are many distinct possibilities, but few conclusive answers.

Late in the Classic Pueblo Period came the most intriguing cultural change. For reasons again open to considerable speculation, all over the Four Corners area many of the Anasazi began to move into canyon cliff alcoves. There they built quite fine masonry dwellings, some of the larger villages constructed out of stone and timbers dismantled from mesa top pueblos, and occasionally set atop the filled-in remains of earlier pithouses. Most of these cliff dwellings were easily defensible, and some were well-hidden and all but inaccessible, again raising the idea that the Ancient Ones were afraid of some form of attack. Yet there is little evidence that such fears were ever realized.

Whether the reason for this dramatic shift in residence location was caused by internal or external strife—or neither—this change was accomplished over a relatively short span of time. It was a laborious task to build in such difficult locations. Retaining walls usually had to be built and filled in with dirt and rubble to level cave floors. The stone, lumps of clay, twigs and bark, jars of water for making mortar, and posts for roof and ladder construction, all had to be transported to the caves. Despite all the effort expended, the Anasazi did not remain long in these unusual abodes. The cliff dwellers inhabited their alcove homes for only fifty to one hundred fifty years. Then began the time known as the Cultural Decline.

DOOR DETAIL – LION HOUSE
Access to rooms in Anasazi dwellings was normally through small, window-sized apertures, either rectangular or T-shaped. In some cases roof hatchways were used.

MORRIS 5
This wall shows excellent masonry typical of many Classic Pueblo rooms. Sandstone blocks were roughly shaped with hammerstones, then the bricks were pecked and smoothed.

Around A.D. 1276, a drought began which lasted until the end of the century. Although this dry period was not much worse than previous ones had been, it was to prove the end for Anasazi occupation of the Mesa Verde region. For too many generations, with an ever-increasing population, the Ancient Ones had lived in a land unable to support great numbers—at least not without a good crop yield. The climate had also grown somewhat colder; growing seasons were shortened. And with trees and brush cut down for fuel and construction and to clear fields for planting, there was little root system to hold the dirt. Because of the lack of vegetation, most of the game animals had left the area. And even before that particular drought, the climate had been dryer than usual. Without sufficient rain and snow for the cultivated fields, survival became impossible.

Many factors undoubtedly contributed to the decline of the civilization, but the Anasazi did not suddenly come to the decision to migrate; the abandonment of the area was quite gradual. Those cave villagers of Lion Canyon, in fact, apparently left their homes some forty to fifty years before their neighbors in the great cliff dwellings of the National Park decided it was time to move on.

Contrary to popular myth, the Anasazi did not simply disappear. Their descendants live on in the Pueblos of contemporary Arizona and New Mexico, but never again was the Mesa Verde-Mancos Canyon area occupied by so large a farming culture. The ruins of that fascinating Stone Age civilization were to sit in empty silence for many generations before they would be appreciated and the builders of that long-ago society accorded the respect and recognition they deserve.

ANTIQUITIES LAWS

Anasazi ruins and artifacts are protected by Federal, State, and Ute Mountain Tribal Park laws. Serious penalties are in store for anyone who willfully defaces, destroys, or removes anything of archaeological value. One of the special joys of this park is the rare opportunity to see artifacts just as they were left behind by the Ancient Ones. Examine them as you wish, take as many pictures as you desire, then leave them where they are. This law applies, as well, to anything found lying about away from ruin sites, such as potsherds or arrow points. Think twice before taking that pretty pottery piece you find; Tribal law enacts a $500.00 fine for the removal of a single potsherd. Enjoy what you find, but do not take anything from the area.

INACCESSIBLE HOUSE

A Personal Experience Essay

The first step is the hardest. A cliched statement but, in this instance, how true. For you must go over the edge of the cliff, lean out with your rear, brace yourself against the rock, and put trust in your equipment. The only way into Inaccessible House is by rope, rappelling into and later out of the cliff village. And it will definitely be worth the effort, for this alcove home of the Ancient Ones sits on a narrow ledge, brooding and silent, almost invisible from below, and unreachable by any other method.

I tell myself these things, go over them all in my mind, seeking reassurance, but still the thought of that first step causes the stomach to flutter, the heart to race, sweat to bead the forehead and grease the palms of the hands. I peek over the cliff edge to see the Ute Tribal Park pickup, a tiny white speck some seven hundred feet below in the depths of Navajo Canyon. Of course I tell myself that the sheer part of the cliff is only about eighty feet in height. The rest is slope. Steep slope, rocky and brush covered. Very steep slope. I find no consolation there, either.

I have rappelled before with my son, John, a climber of a few years experience. But never off a cliff like this one, knowing that I will be required to do a hanging rappel, away from the rock, something new for me. Once past the lip of the alcove in which nestles Inaccessible House, I must move down freely, past the floor level of the cliff village, until the rope above my head can be caught and, like a helpless fish, I will be hauled inside the cave.

Simple. I could do it. Others have been brought to this special place, and returned safely. NOTE: Inaccessible House is only toured by request, but let it be completely understood, it is not necessary to go to these lengths to fully enjoy the park and what it has to offer. To have this kind of opportunity is appealing to some, and is the reason for including this account.

"You don't have to do this, Mother," John says, after I voice my fear. A trace of nervousness is detected in his tone, also.

"Yes, I do. It's something I want to do for myself, just to know that I did it." My voice is shaking somewhat, but there is no mistaking my determination, and John gives no argument.

My son has brought along his own climbing gear, including plenty of carabiners, lengths of webbing, two ropes. And we each have our own harness. Preparing, he insists that one of those ropes be attached to me as a safety line. How fortunate. I was soon to learn how wise that precaution was.

A deep breath while willing my heart not to beat so loud, and that first step is taken. The rope runs through the brake in front of me, held above with my right hand. The remainder of the rope passes around my back, over my left thigh and between my legs from the front, to disappear out of sight below. Yes, I take that first step--but nothing happens. I give the rope a tug, prepared to take another step down the rock face. Still, I can go nowhere.

"I can't move," I complain.

My son's reply is curt, again his concern is evidenced.

"I really can't go anywhere," I reiterate, voice rising slightly in frustration.   "The rope won't budge."

"Come back up then," John says.

HIKING TO MESA TOP
With all equipment necessary for rappelling, a steep climb is made to the top of Chapin Mesa, above Inaccessible House.   There is a rise in elevation of some 700 feet, from canyon bottom to mesa top.

Oh sure! Come back up. Once to take that first step is hard enough, but to repeat it! Come back up, he says. Awkwardly, I obey. Scrambling over the sloping rim, I straighten up, return my point of balance to my feet. My legs tremble slightly.

John checks the brake, a system of six carabiners linked in a special way, a method favored by many climbers. The doubled rope that runs through the brake had somehow become crossed, not allowing it to slide freely. Better to have had that happen near the top, I decide, instead of twenty-five feet down the rock. A quick adjustment is made and back over the edge I go.

Maybe that first step is the hardest, but the second beginning is not much easier. Just don't look down, I tell myself. Concentrate on the rock before you. Lean out, keep the knees flexible, feet perpendicular to the rock. Just walk down backwards. One step at a time, slide the rope through, right hand above the brake pulling gently, left one holding the rope at the side of my waist.

This is fun! Easy. No harder than other rappels I have done. This wall is just straight up and down and my destination can't be seen, that's all. Nothing to it. I begin to really enjoy myself. I'm not one to rush a rappel, though, to take bounding leaps down the rock like some fond of the sport are wont to do. Step by step I lower my body down. Ten, twenty, thirty feet. The lip of the alcove is reached and without hesitation I step off the rock. Hanging free, what a sensation! Nothing but the rope attached above, belayed by my son, to defy the tug of gravity. My feet dangle down now, the rope and brake are directly in front of my head.

Arthur Cuthair, Park Director and our guide

for the day, had taken my camera with him on his descent. He leans out of the alcove, braces himself against a masonry wall of Inaccessible House, and says, "Stay there. Let me take your picture."

Looking over my right shoulder, I give a broad smile, thinking: What an angle for a picture! The camera pointed straight up, my rear prominent to the lens, with the climbing harness tight around my thighs, pulled taut by the rope that holds me in the air.

"Got it!" Arthur says.

I swing my head back to the front, prepared to return to the matter of descending the final ten feet. I start to slide the rope through the brake, but something is again wrong. When my head swung around a large clump of hair had caught in the doubled rope, just below the brake. My downward tug pulled that swatch of hair into the brake itself. I try to free it by holding myself dangling in space with one hand. But I'm not strong enough, and slip further. My hair is hopelessly entangled now, the brake pulled tight against my scalp at the right temple.

There is no time to panic. I have to shout to be heard, but my voice is strangely calm. "John! I have a problem. My hair's caught in the brake. You'll have to pull me back up a ways."

It's hard to be heard, to be understood, by someone on top of the cliff and back from the edge. Somehow, John hears and comprehends. My son is not a large man. One hundred and forty pounds at best. But with the safety rope (God bless him forever for his foresight) he is able to pull me up, far enough that I can put my toes above the lip of the alcove, lean in, straighten up, paste myself to the rock wall. With my weight distributed between several points, my left hand clutching the safety line, I am able to free the pull against the rappelling rope. Quickly, I extricate my lock of hair from the brake.

A huge sigh of relief escapes as tension rushes from me. I am not to be scalped on the Indian reservation after all, a joke I share with Arthur later in the day. In fact, it is not really until much later that I fully realize how close I came to a very nasty, painful, and possibly dangerous injury.

"O.K." I yell upwards. "I'm going down again." And proceed to do so, with no further mishap. Past the lip of the cave, swinging free once again, on down, more careful with my hair this time, you can be sure.

"Just a little farther," Arthur says, by way of encouragement, his round face wearing a big grin.

I go slightly beyond the alcove floor level; Arthur leans out and catches the rope above my head, then swings me inward. My feet reach out, touch solid ground; I stand up and give a big whoop. "Made it!" I say, or something equally inane.

What a thrill! The excitement of the entire episode fills me, can barely be contained. My adrenalin is pumping. The thought of what might have happened up there if the thick lock of hair had been plucked from my scalp does not concern me. For the moment, it is forgotten.

I move off along the narrow ledge where the Anasazi chose to build what is now called Inaccessible House, work my way through a few tiny rubble-filled rooms. The alcove ledge curves outward. I am at a good angle for pictures of my

son as he rappels into the cliff village. Because
of my position within the alcove, he will not come
into sight until just before the hanging part of
the descent. I wait in place, leaning out over
the edge with no thought to my safety. I feel so
elated, so absolutely fearless at that moment, and
the pictures taken of John are terrific.

THE RAPPEL

*John Akens, as he nears the hanging portion
of the rappel into Inaccessible House. The
village, all but invisible in the shadows, lies on
a narrow ledge.*

All within the cave, we explore from room to room and level to level--no easy task where floors, ceilings have collapsed, to leave piles of stone and fallen timbers. Rather than work my way down two stories, then back up, I choose to follow Arthur along the top of a room's outer wall, where one slip, one moment of vertigo, might tip me over the edge into the canyon. But I feel invincible, there is no thought of danger. Greater than the thrill of the moment, however, is a deep feeling of personal satisfaction, fulfillment, an emotion so strong I wish it could be kept with me forever, to be recalled at will and savored when needed.

John, Arthur, and I marvel how anyone could have lived in such an isolated place. What fear drove the inhabitants of this small village to seclude themselves on a ledge no wider at any given point than ten, fifteen feet? How dangerous it must have been to live here, especially if there were young children among the residents. A portion of the ledge collapsed at some time in the past, centuries ago perhaps, plunging part of the dwellings to the canyon below. I study the remaining section of ledge, only three or four feet of rock, and wonder if the village was occupied at the time.

Another question comes to mind. How did those people get in and out of their town? Certainly they did not enter and exit as we are required to do. Perhaps the collapsed part of the ledge provided the answer. Maybe there were toe and finger holds in the rock that we can no longer find evidence of. Yet it is another thirty feet or so to a narrow, slanting rock outcropping below the cave, that provides a way to descend to the base of the cliff wall and the beginning of the rocky slope. I mull these questions in my mind but find no answers. Perhaps they are questions that will never be answered.

We sit on the narrowest part of the ledge
where our view is unobstructed and take lunch from
our day packs. Eating quietly, we enjoy the broad
vistas before us, our gaze traveling across the
canyon to the opposite cliffs, up into the blue-
bright sky, or down into the chasm far below.
Silence reigns, deep and profound, until we hear
the raucous caw of a sleek-winged raven, then
again it is still. A scant few miles up the
canyon from where we sit is the Mesa Verde
National Park museum, where on a summer day such
as this, hundreds to thousands of visitors view
the relics of this vanished civilization we find
so fascinating, gaze in wonder at Spruce Tree
House, or go down the trail to that gem of a
cliff dwelling. That multitude of chattering
tourists might as well be on another planet, as
far as we are concerned. In our world, there are
only the three of us, and we are content that it
is so.

It's soon time to leave, however.
Reluctantly, we prepare. "You want to go first
this time?" Arthur asks of me.

"Sure." My reply is instantaneous, given
with no reservation. I'm an old hand at this now.
Euphoria fills me with confidence. I could do
most anything at that moment. I rope up, ready
myself. The next stage of the descent is nearly
as long as the first, but will involve no hanging
rappel. I can lead the way this time.

I step out, and back--to a surprise. Arthur
didn't explain that where I am making my egress is
ten feet farther away from where we came into the
cave. The rope, still attached above, is now at
an angle. My body swings sideways, my feet are
unable to gain purchase on the rock. "Whoo!" I
shout. "You didn't tell me this would happen!"
My cry is not one of alarm, there is no
remonstrance in my tone. Common sense should have

told me that my body would have to swing over until I was directly beneath the rope. Besides, it's kind of fun, I discover.

My body weight stabilized again, I walk on down the cliff. My going is swifter this time, for I am trying out a different kind of brake, the one Arthur used earlier. The rope moves through it more quickly, making it hard to hold myself in one place. I soon come to the narrow ledge that slants to the cliff base. Without this convenient ledge, we could not reach the bottom, for the rope would not be long enough.

I untie the rope from my harness, the others haul it up to use for their own descent. John is next, Arthur the last to leave the village. On the path below I take pictures of them as they come down, Arthur really getting into the action of the swing, hamming it up for the camera.

Arthur lies down for a nap, his hat pulled low to shade his face. John goes around the mesa point to climb the jumbled rocks on the far side-- the only place of access to the top--to retrieve his climbing gear. Restless, I move off along the trail at the cliff base to await my son's return. Finding a shaded spot, I sit down. Alone, I look out over the canyon and revel in the silence, allow my delight in the experience just past to wash over me. For it has proved to be a true adventure, of the flesh, of the spirit.

Ahead of me, there is still the long hike down the steep switchbacks of the trail to the canyon bottom, out in the merciless heat of an August afternoon, then the bone-jarring miles of four-wheeling to where the mouth of Navajo Canyon opens into the Mancos River gorge, and on to the Ute Tribal Park campground. None of that is on my mind. My head seems emptied of thoughts. Time and space are relative. There is no yesterday, no tomorrow. There is just now, just here, just me and this vast, silent canyon, the sandstone cliff hard against my back, the sky an empty blue bowl overhead. And there is peace, tranquillity, complete.

INACCESSIBLE HOUSE
Only minor stabilization has been done in this remote, difficult to visit, cliff dwelling. Rubble and fallen timbers fill the tiny rooms.

HISTORY OF
ARCHAEOLOGICAL DISCOVERY

It is not known who might have been the first white man to discover the prehistoric ruins of the Mesa Verde. The Spanish priest and explorer, Escalante, camped nearby with his party in August of 1776. Although he is often credited with the naming of the "Rio de los Mancos," Escalante made no mention in his diary of the mesa or its ruins.

In 1873, miners began to enter the region in search of precious metals, mainly gold and silver. John Moss was such a prospector. He gave the Utes a bagful of trinkets to show his amiability and good intentions, in return for which he was given twenty-five square miles in the La Plata foothills, with the guarantee that he could prospect there without interference from the Indians. Apparently the "land grant" given Moss by the Utes failed to produce much of value and Moss moved on, in search of a more lucrative area. His travels took him through the Mancos Valley and on into the canyon. It was there that he later said he noted--without much apparent interest-- several small dwellings in the cliff alcoves high above the river. He then returned to the La Plata area.

A year later, in 1874, Mr. William Henry Jackson, who later became known as the "Pioneer Photographer," came into the region. Jackson, taking pictures for the Hayden geographical and geological survey teams, visited the La Plata mining district, where he began to hear stories about the ancient ruins of the Mesa Verde. Intrigued, Jackson hired the man from whom the stories had originated, the aforementioned John Moss. The prospector agreed to guide Jackson and his small party to the ruins he had seen in the cliffs bordering the Mancos River Canyon.

The first day out--as one version of the story goes--evening fell with no sighting of the ruins having been made. Seated around the campfire after dinner, discussion naturally turned to the "supposed" ruins. Everyone was tired and irritable and perhaps beginning to doubt the credibility of their guide. Impatiently, one young man of the party turned to Moss and asked him just where were the ruins they meant to photograph. Without glancing up, John Moss waved one arm in the direction of the cliff and said, "Right up there."

The others looked up. Much to their amazement, there was indeed a ruin visible above the rocky slopes, highlighted by the brilliant rays of the lowering sun. After a steep scramble, Jackson and one other man succeeded in reaching the ruins high in the cliff just as darkness descended. The party returned to the alcove dwelling the next day with their photographic equipment. Named Two Story House by Jackson, his was the first recorded entering of a cliff dwelling by a white man, most certainly it was the first one ever photographed. In the ensuing days, as the survey team moved through the canyon, additional discoveries were made, confined mainly to towers and other surface ruins along the river--all of which are now in Ute Mountain Tribal Park.

A second government survey crew traveled through the region in 1875. William H. Holmes, assistant geologist, visited the much larger ruin known as Sixteen Window House, where he collected a few pieces of pottery that were later sent to the National Museum. This cliff dwelling is

designated on the map contained in the Ute Tribal
Park brochure. It can be seen with binoculars
from the road beyond the Johnson Canyon turnoff.

In 1881, Ben Wetherill and his family settled
in the Mancos Valley on the east side of the Mesa
Verde. It was Ben's sons who were to figure so
prominently in the discovery of the major ruins of
the mesa, both north and south of the river. When
the Wetherills switched from farming to running
cattle, their Alamo (Spanish for Cottonwood) Ranch
grew quickly. Due to heavy snows in the Mancos
Valley and increasing size of their herd, it
became necessary to seek winter range elsewhere.
The Wetherills had always been on good terms with
the Utes, both having learned to trust and respect
the other. It was this special relationship that
allowed the Wetherills to winter their cattle in
Mancos Canyon and its many branches.

Around 1884 or 1885, the Wetherills built a
cabin (or perhaps merely a shelter, as no remains
of any structure have been found) at the mouth of
Johnson Canyon. During their stay at the cabin,
Ben's sons Richard and Al, and son-in-law Charles
Mason, often relieved their boredom by looking for
Indian ruins, at that time locally--and
mistakenly--called "Aztec ruins."

An elderly Ute by the name of Acowitz lived
near the Wetherills. He approached Richard one
day and hesitantly told him of the many large
ruins hidden in the canyons of the Mesa Verde.
*"One of those ruins...is bigger than all the
rest,"* Acowitz said. Since the area was held
sacred by the Utes, the old Indian refused to go
there or say more about the exact location. This
small bit of fascinating information, however, was
to lead to the eventual discovery of Cliff Palace,
followed quickly by Spruce Tree House and Square
Tower Ruin, all major attractions in Mesa Verde
National Park. These exciting finds were to

foster in Richard Wetherill a consuming interest in Anasazi ruins, one that would last his lifetime.

Torn between ranch duties and their passion for the ruins, the Wetherill boys worked summer and fall at the ranch and devoted the winter months to their search for ruins. In December of 1889, the brothers and Charles Mason set out, this time to Johnson Canyon--mainly the Lion Canyon branch--where they excavated many cliff dwellings.

TREE HOUSE
Students from the University of New Mexico, Las Cruces, explore the village of Tree House, the first cliff dwelling visited on the Main Ruins tour. The two people in the center are examining a boulder in which Al and John Wetherill carved their names and dates of visit. The Wetherill name is synonymous with early exploration and excavation in the region.

It was in fortified House, which can be viewed on the Main Ruins tour by walking along Lion Canyon rim, that John Wetherill made an important find. The thrill of discovery is reflected in his diary account: *"Glancing up I noticed a door that had been concealed...I removed a rock and saw that it was the only entrance."* After he removed a section of the room's wall down to the floor level, John's shovel uncovered pieces of burial matting. When the rubbish was cleared away he found a piece of belt. *"It was three-colored, red, white, and black."* John Wetherill then broke through a wall on another side, dug to the floor and uncovered more matting. *"I removed some dirt and found an arrow with an agate point on it, the first ever found in a cliff dwelling in Mancos Canyon."*

John then called to Mason and together they excavated the room. His narration continued, *"Charley removed two or three shovelfuls of dirt and dug out a basket."* Their finds then came quickly. *"We found seventeen arrows lying across the heads of five bodies. Between the skulls were four bowls. One large skeleton lay on top of the mat with a bow on one side, a mug and a basket on the other. He had nothing over him; a pair of moccasins on his feet and some feather cloth under his head."* Near him they found a hollow stick with both ends wrapped with sinew. The approximately twenty inch stick had a bone point at one end which measured about six inches long.

"Lying alongside of this body were the skeletons of three babies...two of them had pieces of buckskin with them." After taking up these bodies, they found a large mat which covered the entire floor. *"We removed this and found another skeleton and a stick with a loop at the end, that we took for a medicine stick, also two prairie dog skin pouches. The skeleton was covered with a willow mat. Under the mat were two more made of*

*grass. Under the grass mat was one of feather
cloth, after that a buckskin jacket with fringes."*
The latter find was rare indeed in this--or any
other--area.

FORTIFIED HOUSE
*As seen from the west rim of Lion Canyon,
this ruin contained numerous burials unearthed
during Wetherill exploration of the Johnson Canyon
area.*

After working through Lion and Johnson
Canyons, the brothers and Charles Mason returned
to Cliff Palace. By March of the following year,
1890, Richard Wetherill, either alone or with his
family, had found and examined all of the major
cliff dwellings in the Mesa Verde. Although they
are often criticized as "pothunters," all early
attempts made by the Wetherills to interest the
scientific community in the Mesa Verde ruins fell
on deaf ears. Southwestern archaeology was in its
infancy. And although their methods may have been

somewhat crude, the Wetherills did much toward bringing knowledge of the Anasazi to public awareness.

THE WETHERILL BROTHERS
Courtesy of Colorado Historical Society - F15989

Seated: Alfred, Richard, and John
Standing: Winslow and Clayton
The picture was taken at their Alamo Ranch in the Mancos Valley, east of the Mesa Verde.

There were others during this time with great interest in the region's ruins. One person important to the history of the Mesa Verde was Virginia McClurg, a correspondent for the New York Graphic. She first came to Durango in 1882, to investigate lost cities of the prehistoric Southwest. A localized Ute uprising that year prevented her search. she returned again in 1885, but was able to visit only a few small ruins. McClurg decided to come back again in 1886, this time accompanied by a guide and photographer. Her explorations took her into some of the lower canyons that emptied into the Mancos. There she made several important finds, including Balcony House, now a favorite of tourists who visit the National Park.

Between 1887 and 1906, Virginia McClurg launched a continuous--and ultimately successful--campaign to see to the preservation of the cliff dwellings of the Mesa Verde. Negotiations were even made with Chief Ignacio for the ruins to be protected, with the Utes retaining the grazing rights to the land.

In 1897, McClurg was joined in her battle to protect the ancient ruins by the Colorado Federation of Women's Clubs, spearheaded by a committee of fourteen dedicated women. In three years this group had expanded into the Colorado Cliff Dwellers Association. The year 1901 saw McClurg and her organization take control of the ruins. In return, they paid the Utes a nominal fee of $300.00.

President Theodore Roosevelt signed the bill that created Mesa Verde National Park in 1906. The boundaries were vague, however, and attached to the bill was a hastily drawn amendment that added that "any ruins within five miles of the proposed park" would be included. Two years later, in 1908, the Utes expressed the desire to secure the Ute Mountain Tract, a section of the Montezuma National Forest southwest of Cortez. New negotiations began. The land the Indians wished to trade was of little value to them at the time, as it had no marketable timber and was rough and arid. But it did contain the largest and most important cliff dwellings, which were desired by the government. Several years passed, during which various problems had to be resolved. An agreement was finally submitted to Congress on January 22, 1913, which gave Mesa Verde National Park an additional 24,500 acres in exchange for 30,400 acres received by the Indians.

Another person of historical and archaeological importance to the Mesa Verde was Gustaf Nordenskiold. A twenty-three year old native of Sweden, he came to the Southwest in 1891 to see the sights and visit a dry, warm climate for his tuberculosis. Nordenskiold heard about the cliff dwellings and decided to see for himself. The summer and autumn he spent in the area, guided by Richard, John, and Al Wetherill, resulted in the 1893 publication of a book authored by the young Swede, entitled THE CLIFF DWELLERS OF THE MESA VERDE. Some of the best descriptions and early-day photographs of the region and its ruins can be found in this classic volume. He was also taken to visit the Lion and Johnson Canyon ruins, but he did not carry out any excavations, merely took pictures. What might possibly be the first photograph ever taken of the Tribal Park's "Eagle's Nest" cliff dwelling is included in his book.

Nordenskiold did much collecting of artifacts. Since there were as yet no laws to prevent him from doing otherwise, he left the country with a valuable collection. This now resides in the National Museum of Finland, where it is kept in storage. Despite the loss of much Mesa Verde archaeological material, the young man must be commended for the manner in which he detailed his finds. Nordenskiold's work was extensive and, for those times, quite scientific.

Earl Morris, a noted early Southwestern archaeologist, visited the Johnson Canyon region in 1913. He carried out more thorough excavations in some Lion Canyon cliff dwellings than had the Wetherill brothers before him. In 1929, he returned to the area to excavate a large village on the mesa above Johnson Canyon, where several exciting finds were made. Others did work in the region, also, in 1935, 1958, and in 1967. It was not until 1972 to 1976, however, that an archaeological survey of any extent was made, this for the proposed Tribal Park. Partial excavation was also carried out, to prepare for the tours. David A. Breternitz of the University of Colorado was the director of that extensive undertaking.

MORRIS 5
This kiva was excavated by the University of Colorado. Note the original roof beams.

NATURAL ENVIRONMENT
FLORA
(And How it was Utilized by the Anasazi)

There are three factors which determine where certain plant species will grow: soil, moisture, and temperature. Although there is some natural over-lapping of species, in general the plant communities that flourish at higher elevations of the Mesa Verde will differ from those found in the canyons and along the Mancos River. The Ute Tribal Park has several distinct plant communities; major classifications include the Pinyon-Juniper Forest, Big Sagebrush, and the River, or Riparian. At first glance, the appearance of much of the area might indicate that little of value grows here, as far as human utilization of vegetation goes. On the contrary, the study of Anasazi trash accumulations and the artifacts associated with their habitations shows that the Ancient Ones made use of a wide variety of plant species.

The predominant plant community of the highlands, both north and south of the river, is the Pinyon-Juniper Forest, although in the upper elevations and at the heads of some canyons may be found stands of the taller trees, the douglas fir, aspen, and ponderosa pine. All three provided useful timber for the construction of Anasazi villages. The douglas fir was the preferred wood for roofing beams, due to its strength and long, straight growth form, although aspen was also used as both primary and secondary roof beams. Ponderosa pine appeared to be popular in the form of split planks.

THE TALL TREES

Thick stands of douglas fir and ponderosa pine often thrive in moist areas at canyon heads or where run-off is greatest. This particular group hides Fortified House from view.

The short-needled pinyon pine tree supplied much of the firewood and roofing materials for the Ancient Ones. Every few years, provided there was sufficient moisture, this squat member of the pine family gave the Anasazi something they undoubtedly cherished even more, a crop of delectable nuts, not only flavorful, but rich in protein. The pine nuts were roasted, then eaten plain or ground into flour. Pinyon pitch, or gum as it is also called, is the sticky substance that oozes from the trees. It was used to waterproof baskets and repair cracks in pottery. In some contemporary Pueblo Indian societies, after a death occurs, the pitch is burned so that the cleansing vapors can be inhaled as protection against sorcery, a custom perhaps handed down from Anasazi ancestors.

The Utah juniper, often mistakenly called a cedar, is a stubby, twisted, shaggy-barked tree, with scale-like leaves or needles. It produces gray-green berries which can be used as a food supplement, as flavoring, or for medicinal purposes. The Ancient Ones used the large seeds from the berries for the making of jewelry. Bark from the juniper was shredded and used for stuffing, weaving, or padding, or tied together to form a ring and used as a jar support for their rounded-bottom pottery vessels. Like its companion species the pinyon, the Utah juniper was used as firewood, for tool and weapon making, and for home construction. It was highly regarded for roof support beams as it is structurally stronger than pine and more commonly found than the taller trees.

UPPER SODA CANYON
In the upper reaches of canyons, the Pinyon-Juniper Forest Community is prevalent. This is also true of the surrounding mesa tops.

Soil of the Pinyon-Juniper forest is normally rich and fertile, with fairly deep loam. It contains red loess, a wind-deposited soil that is excellent for agriculture, a factor which certainly appealed to the Ancient Ones. Since the natural vegetation also thrives in a Pinyon-Juniper Forest Community, the task of clearing the land for planting must have been monumental, given the limited tools available to the Anasazi farmer. The trees had to be cut down with stone axes. The stumps were then undoubtedly burned, after which they were pried loose with digging sticks. If too difficult to remove, the dead stumps were left in place. Wherever possible, all the native plants were removed from field areas, for nothing could be allowed to compete with cultivated crops for precious moisture.

The second major plant community of the park is called the Big Sagebrush. There is sometimes a distinct line of demarcation between the Pinyon-Juniper and Big Sagebrush communities. The latter is the predominant one in the canyons. Among, but certainly not limited to, the most useful plants associated with the Big Sagebrush Community are the serviceberry, Oregon grape, chokecherry, mock orange, squawbush, the Mormon tea, Gambel oak, cliffrose, yucca, and various cacti. All of these were utilized by the Ancient Ones.

The silvery-green sagebrush (not to be confused with the herb sage) is an important plant of the canyon bottom floodplains. Sagebrush can also be found in areas of the mesa top where the soil is deep and free of alkali, often occurring in large stands. It is also associated with "disturbed" areas, such as Anasazi ruins. The sagebrush was burned copiously in prehistoric times, and undoubtedly the Ancient Ones were aware of its medicinal properties. A tea brewed from its pungent leaves is used as a cure for many ailments by modern Indian societies; it is considered to be especially beneficial for coughs, colds, and indigestion.

Common throughout the area is the serviceberry shrub. After the early-blooming, five-petaled white flowers appear, the serviceberry produces edible fruit, although it is usually somewhat dry and tasteless in this region, due to the aridity. This small fruit, blue to purple in color, resembles the blueberry, but it is more closely related to the apple. It can be eaten fresh, dried whole, or pounded and spread into cakes to dry. In the latter form it can be made into pemmican.

Creeping Oregon grape, or barberry, is a low dwarf evergreen shrub found in shaded side canyons where the soil is moist. The holly-like leaves

LOWER SODA CANYON
In the lower elevations of canyons is seen the beginning of the Big Sagebrush Community, and its accompanying plant species.

are especially attractive in the fall, when they turn shades of red, yellow, or purple. Clusters of tiny flowers mature into blue berries in late autumn. These were probably eaten both raw by the Anasazi and used in pemmican. The leaves and stems are also useful, for from them a good rheumatism medicine can be made.

One of the larger shrubs is the chokecherry. Like the Oregon grape, it grows only in moist areas of the Big Sagebrush Community. Creamy white flowers of the chokecherry hang in clusters. The fruit, usually ripe in August, consists of a small dark red cherry with a large pit. This somewhat sour fruit can be eaten raw, dried for later use, or pounded and made into cakes. Many contemporary people make chokecherry jam. The wood from the chokecherry was also quite popular with the Ancient Ones. It was favored for the making of bows.

The mock orange, or fendlerbush, is a common shrub found most often in the southern parts of the Mesa Verde. It has narrow leaves and large, showy four-petaled white flowers that give off a citrus fragrance that resembles orange, lemon, or even pineapple. The fruit, although small, is edible. Stems from this erect shrub were popular with the Anasazi for the making of arrowshafts.

Squawbush, as the skunkbush sumac is commonly called, has a strong odor, especially when the leaves are rubbed between the fingers. It is also referred to as the "lemonade" bush, for the red berries produced by the plant can be made into a drink. They can also be eaten fresh. Although the berry is slightly sticky and somewhat acid to the taste, it is not unpalatable. A few of these popped into the mouth on a hot day releases saliva and lessens thirst. Twigs from the squawbush were used by Indian women (hence the name) in the construction of baskets and cradleboards, a practice which continues in contemporary Native American societies.

Another plant common to the lower elevations of the Mesa Verde is Mormon, or Brigham, tea. A medicinal drink can be brewed from the jointed yellow to green stems, which is said to aid in the cure of such diverse ailments as venereal disease, kidney infection, coughs, and stomach disorders. It is also enjoyed simply for its flavor, although for some people the tea is an acquired taste. This member of the ephedra family also contains much tannin, making it useful in the preparation of animal hides. Its seeds can be roasted, then eaten plain or ground into meal.

The Gambel, or scrub, oak is an indicator of moist soil. Its dense growth provides cover and browse for deer. Indians used the wood for dwelling construction, as digging sticks, and to make bows. Another weapon made from scrub oak was the throwing club (similar to a non-returning boomerang) used in hunting rabbits. Acorns from the Gambel oak were roasted, pounded, and mixed with dried meat or fat. These scrub oak acorns are less bitter tasting than ones from others in that plant family, and require less leeching to make them palatable.

An especially showy plant is the cliffrose, with its tiny leaves and abundant white-to-yellow flowers that effuse a musky fragrance. This June-to-August blooming shrub is most commonly found on mesa rims and canyon sides. Although the plant's foliage can be brewed into an acceptable tea, it is also used medicinally. A potion made from the leaves and twigs induces vomiting, to purge the system. The Anasazi used the wood of the cliffrose for the making of arrows and other tools, and the stringy bark of older specimens was braided into cord or mats. After it has blossomed, this wild member of the rose family can be recognized by its display of clematis-like feathery tails.

The Ancient Ones found the yucca, both broad-leaf and narrow-leaf, to be one of the most useful of nature's gifts. Flower stalks of the yucca are edible, as are the waxy white petals of its tulip-like blossoms. The fleshy green fruit can be eaten raw, cooked down to a thick paste, or dried for later use. The large black seeds can be roasted and eaten whole or ground into flour. Soap comes from the yucca root, and from the leaves the Anasazi got the fiber to weave cordage, mats, baskets, nets, and all manner of clothing and sandals.

BROADLEAF YUCCA

All parts of the yucca, both broadleaf and narrow leaf, were utilized by the Anasazi--stalk, flowers, leaves, roots, and seeds. It was considered one of Nature's most useful gifts. This particular plant was photographed beside the Main Ruins trail, near the cliff dwellings.

To prepare yucca leaves, those from the center of the plant are gathered, folded into bundles, then dropped into a pot of boiling water. Juniper ashes are added, after which the leaves are ready to be peeled and chewed or pounded. Following the separation of the leaves, the fiber is tied in small bundles for later use. Many of these "quids," as archaeologists call prepared bundles of yucca fibers, are found during excavation of ruins. Since some nutritional benefit can be derived from the chewing of these quids, they might also be considered a food source. The tip of the yucca leaf also served as paint brush for the application of designs on pottery made by the Anasazi women, a practice still followed by many contemporary Indian artists.

There are many species of cactus found in the park. One fairly common kind is the hedgehog, or claret-cup, with its bright red to violet-purple spring blossoms. The fruit of this small round cactus can be eaten or used medicinally. Collected in the spring, the hedgehog cactus can be dried for use as a sweetener. This plant, which normally grows in clumps of from a few to several hundred, is a prime example of "overlapping," for it is also found frequently in the Pinyon-Juniper Forest Community.

Another cactus useful to the Anasazi and abundant at the lower elevations is the prickly-pear. This easily recognized plant, with its spiny, flat, jointed stems, has large yellow or violet spring and summer flowers, which develop into tasty cylindrical greenish-yellow or reddish fruit. Both the fruit and fleshy stems still are favorite foods of Indians and others who live in the Southwest. Once the spines have been burned or rolled off, the prickly-pear can be eaten raw, roasted, stewed, or dried and ground into meal. Several varieties of this cactus grow in the Big

Sagebrush Community; one especially attractive to watch for has flowers that fade from yellow to orange as the blossom matures.

Beside the river is found still another plant community, the Riparian. Although the Mancos is a perennial stream with unreliable water flow except during spring snow-melt in the La Plata Mountains and after heavy late summer rains, certain plants do grow there that are seldom seen elsewhere in the park. The Fremont cottonwood is an example. Related to the poplar and willow, the cottonwood is a water-loving tree. Some of the Fremont Cottonwoods are virtual giants, attaining a height of ninety feet with a diameter of five feet. Artifacts made from cottonwood trees were found during excavation of Lion House; the Navajo favor the wood for the making of many things, from prayersticks to dice.

The boxelder is another common tree in the Riparian Community. It often rivals the cottonwood in size. A type of maple, the boxelder produces a sap which can be boiled down to a sweet syrup, although it is not known whether the Anasazi utilized it as such. Artifacts made from this wood have also been found in Lion Canyon cliff dwellings.

Another species that grows primarily in this community is the willow, although it can be found wherever ground water is abundant and close to the surface. The slender branches of the willow were, and still are, highly regarded by Indian women for basket weaving. The Anasazi also made tools from willow wood, and it was one of the species inserted into masonry walls to serve as pegs on which to hang things, from strips of drying meat to personal belongings such as clothing.

Fourwing saltbush is another important species that is most often associated with the

River Community, where it frequently occurs in pure stands. Leaves from the saltbush, or its close relation the shadscale, are used as a seasoning. The tender young leaves of spring, while not yet as salty tasting as they will be later in the year, can be cooked as greens or added to stews. Saltbush ashes make an acceptable substitute for baking powder and perhaps were used as such by the Ancient Ones.

TAMARISK

Tamarisk line the Mancos River. In many areas, this introduced species has forced out the native plant population.

Many tamarisk line the river bank. This small tree is not native to the Southwest and was unknown to the Anasazi. The species is only included here because it is so abundant. Tamarisk was introduced to this country from mid-eastern deserts, such as Arabia, about a century ago. A great deal of the natural vegetation along most Southwestern waterways has been replaced by the fast-spreading tamarisk, for it uses much of the available water. Access to the Mancos River is limited along most of its length through the Tribal Park, especially near the campground, due to thick stands of this tree.

Other species of plants, both common and uncommon, are found within the park, many of which were used by the Anasazi in some form or another. One for which there seems to be little use also deserves mention--and a word of warning. That is poison ivy. This low-growing plant is found along the cool, moist bases of cliffs. The bright green plant, with its typical "leaves of three," is found in several places beside the narrow Lion Canyon Main Ruins trail. Do your best to avoid contact with the skin; the resultant rash can be quite severe.

POISON IVY
This noxious--although quite lovely--plant grows in moist areas at the cliff base along the Main Ruins trail. Be wary!

WILDFLOWERS

Numerous species of wildflowers abound in Ute Mountain Tribal Park, especially in spring and early summer, although certain species, like the purple-hued sticky aster and golden rabbitbrush do not bloom until late summer and early fall. Indian paintbrush, fleabane, yellow salsify, globemallow, prince's plume, several varieties of evening primrose, perky Sue, Eaton penstemon, James Beardstongue, scarlet gilia, and many others, all add splashes of color to the landscape in their season, to rival the flowering yucca, cactus, and shrubs. If you are in the park during blooming periods, enjoy the display, but please leave the flowers for others to do likewise.

EVENING PRIMROSE

YELLOW SALSIFY

FLEABANE

64

FAUNA

Although the Mesa Verde is a somewhat isolated uplands region, it has a relatively diverse wildlife population. Each species that calls the area home--whether as full time or seasonal resident--is well adapted to the environment. Whereas plant communities are influenced by soil, moisture, and temperature, they in turn influence the fauna. Animals tend to live in certain preferred habitats related to the vegetation that grows there. As with the plant species, much of the wildlife of the Ute Tribal Park was a valuable resource for the Anasazi. From animals small and large, from birds and pack rats to the largest mammals, the meat, bones, feathers, and hide were often utilized by the prehistoric peoples.

The Rocky Mountain mule deer is the most common of the larger animals to be found in the park. When the Ancient Ones made a kill of this large-eared species, little of the carcass went to waste. The hide was tanned and made into clothing, the bones and antlers were fashioned into tools, and sinew was used for bow strings or as heavy thread. Deer hoofs strung together served as rattles for personal adornment or ceremonial use, and of course, the meat and most of the internal organs were eaten, some of the venison cooked fresh after a kill, and the remainder dried in strips for later use.

Black bear have been seen in the Tribal Park as have, on occasion, an elk or two. The bones of pronghorn antelope have been found in Lion Canyon ruins, but this species is extremely rare in the

area now. A few mountain lion have also been
spotted from time to time, but they keep pretty
much to themselves. Although the Anasazi favored
the bighorn sheep as a food (especially for the
fat), hide, and tool source, there were few left
in the area by historic times. Reintroduced to
the Mesa Verde, their numbers are increasing but
sightings are still infrequent.

ROCKY MOUNTAIN MULE DEER
*Named for its large, mule-like ears, this is
a young deer. The mule deer was favorite prey for
the Anasazi hunter.*

Actually, one of the most common large
mammals found in Ute Mountain Tribal Park would
have been considered a strange apparition indeed
in the time of the Anasazi. For an unestimated
number of wild horses now roam the canyons of the
Mesa Verde. Most of the Utes who once occupied
the Mancos River Canyon kept horses, some of which
wandered off and were never recovered. Through

the generations the equine population grew. It is
a joy to come upon these horses back in some
remote side canyon but, having truly reverted to
the wild, they are difficult to approach. Small
herds of domesticated horses, allowed to roam free
in Mancos Canyon, are sometimes seen near the
campground, but these are fenced off from joining
their counterparts in the wild.

HORSES

*Some domesticated horses roam free in Mancos
Canyon. Others, truly wild for several
generations, inhabit the upper reaches of canyons.*

Next down in size and more common than most
of the larger mammals are the coyote and bobcat.
Bones from both these species have been found in
park ruins, along with pieces of their hide.
Whether they were used as food is not known. The
coyote, whose mournful chorus can often be heard
at night from the campground, figures prominently
in many stories and legends of present day

Indians.   Perhaps some of these tales   originated during the time of the Ancient Ones.

There are a number of small mammals found in the region. Among those that might be seen are the black-tailed jackrabbit, the ever-present cottontail rabbit, Aberts and red squirrel, yellow-bellied marmot, Gunnison's prairie dog, and the Colorado and least chipmunk.   The weasel, ringtail, porcupine, and spotted skunk, plus bats and various rats and mice also inhabit the park. To judge from the bones found in Anasazi living and refuse areas, most of the above-mentioned species were considered useful, contributing food, hide, bone, fur--or quills in the case of the porcupine. And from the abundance of rabbit bones found, it is safe to assume that "rabbit stew" was probably a favorite on the menu of the Ancient Ones.

COTTONTAIL RABBIT
Common throughout the park, the desert cottontail is active both day and night.

Reptiles, especially those belonging to the lizard family, are common throughout the park. Watch for the distinctive collared lizards of which the Baileys, with its bright green and yellow markings, is the most attractive. Collared lizards, although larger than many others in that family, are sometimes difficult to spot. Besides blending well with their surroundings, they have a habit of remaining completely still. Even when they know they have been seen, the collared lizard will frequently not move unless provoked. With a slow approach, therefore, it is possible to get quite close to these unusual lizards, making them a choice photographic target. Smaller lizards are more common, especially the lesser lizard and many-lined skink. The horned lizard (or toad, as it is commonly though erroneously called) is also found.

NORTHERN PLATEAU LIZARD
This small member of the spiny lizard family, seen frequently in the park, is recognized by the wavy cross lines present in both sexes.

Among the snakes of the park are the garter and gopher, the Mesa Verde night snake, and rattlesnakes. If you are concerned about encountering the latter, rest assured that it is far more likely that the normally shy rattlesnake will see you first, and quietly get out of the way, than vice versa. In any case, he will most always let you know if he is around and you are too near.

Many birds call the park home or frequent the area at certain times of the year. The most majestic is the golden eagle, although an occasional Southern bald eagle is also seen. The turkey vulture, with a wing span of five feet or more, migrates into the area as the cold winter weather passes. Between April and October, these red-to-purple headed, dark-bodied birds can be seen riding the air currents above canyons. Rare sightings have also been made of the peregrine falcon. Another of that species, the prairie falcon, is now believed to be more common in the Ute Tribal Park than older records indicate.

The most common of the medium-sized birds are the jays, the stellar, with its crested head and dark blue body color, and the pinyon and scrub jays. Most of the latter two kinds leave the area in summer, however. There are also flocks of ravens, magpies, and crows present in the park, and the hawk family is represented by the goshawk, sharp shinned hawk, and the Cooper's and sparrow hawk. The Western Horned owl and the pygmy owl also live here. Being nocturnal, your best change at spotting members of the owl family is at dusk. Quail are common, seen especially in the river canyon, and numerous pairs of mourning doves frequent the roadsides on the mesa top drive to the Main Ruins area.

Many smaller birds inhabit the forest, the brush covered slopes, or the canyons. Among them

are chickadees, titmice, wrens, towhees, warblers,
and hummingbirds, of which there are the black-
chinned, ruby-throated, and the rufous. Watch
also for the distinctive nests of the cliff
swallow. The gourd-shaped mud homes of this
colorful bird are sometimes seen attached to the
sandstone ceiling above alcove dwellings of the
Anasazi. The cliff swallow is a social bird who
prefers to live in large numbers but, like
swallows elsewhere, these of the Ute Tribal Park
abandon the area each year to winter in South
America.

The turkey which was domesticated by the
Ancient Ones had almost disappeared from the
region by the beginning of the twentieth century.
What few did remain were shot by hunters during
early exploration of the area. The National Park
Service reintroduced the birds to the Mesa Verde
later, but it is unlikely that many, if any, still
survive in the wild.

GEOLOGY

To understand the geologic story of the Mesa Verde area, it is necessary to go back approximately sixty-five million years, to the Cretaceous period at the end of the Mesozoic era. During that time, a vast sea covered much of the region. This ocean rose and fell periodically, fine sediments being deposited with each fluctuation. The mud and impure limestone that settled on the ocean floor eventually compacted and hardened, resulting in a bedrock layer hundreds of feet thick, known as the Mancos shale. It is a gray to dark-gray layer that contains thin beds of sandy grayish-brown limestone and limestone concretions. Mancos shale comprises the slopes and canyon bottom along the river in the western part of the park.

Marine deposited sand was laid down above the Mancos over the next several million years, possibly washed into the area from streams that drained from the southwest during a time that the sea was withdrawing to the northeast. As subsequent seas advanced and retreated, these layers of coarse sands solidified to become the layer called Point Lookout sandstone. This is a white to yellowish-orange layer of cliff-forming fine-grained sandstone. Its lower region contains interbedded thin sandstone and sandy mudstone. Point Lookout cliffs top the Mancos shale. These two strata are exhibited best near the park entrance, in the vicinity of Chimney Rock, recently renamed Jackson Butte.

The Mesa Verde country underwent another change. As the shoreline retreated, much of the

area became swampland. Plant life, lush and
verdant, thrived. When the plants died, they fell
to the bottom of the swamps where they were buried
along with sediments. This sedimentary and
organic material became the series of rock strata
called the Menefee formation. It is this gray to
grayish-orange layer that makes up the canyon
slopes in the Main Ruins area. Vestiges of this
layer also form the wooded tablelands above the
Point Lookout cliffs seen near the park entrance.

JACKSON BUTTE AND MESA VERDE WEST RIM
*Point lookout sandstone caps the escarpment.
A thin layer of the coal bearing menefee formation
forms the tableland above. The slopes are Mancos
shale, a layer only visible in the lower, western
section of the park.*

The organic portion of the Menefee developed
into low grade coal deposits. These can be seen
at the south end of the mesa and are often visible
for miles. In one area on the south side of Grass

Canyon--a southern tributary of the Mancos River and a popular backpacking area--can be found the region that the early settlers named "The Volcanos" because black smoke from burning coal issued from fissures and cracks in the rock. These "blowouts" may have been important to the Ancient Ones as a source of lithic material for tools and pottery temper.

In time the seas returned. Great amounts of very fine-grained beach and dune sand were deposited. These varied in thickness from one hundred to three hundred feet as a result of changing shoreline and the overlapping and interbedding of materials during the oft-repeated process. This massive yellowish-orange to white layer is appropriately called Cliff House sandstone, for this is the rock that eroded into the alcoves where the Anasazi built their homes. Those Lion Canyon dwellings visited on the Main Ruins tour were constructed in excellent examples of the type of alcove commonly found in the Cliff House sandstone formation.

CANYON GEOLOGY
Cliff house layer tops the menefee formation.

GEOLOGY OF THE MESA VERDE

MAJOR TIME PERIODS

ERA	PALEOZOIC (Age of Ancient Life)								MESOZOIC (Age of Medieval Life)			CENOZOIC (Age of Recent Life)	
	570*								230			63	
PERIOD	PRECAMBRIAN	CAMBRIAN	ORDOVICIAN	SILURIAN	DEVONIAN	MISSISSIPPIAN	PENNSYLVANIAN	PERMIAN	TRIASSIC	JURASSIC	CRETACEOUS	TERTIARY	QUARTERNARY

* Numbers indicate millions of years before present

CANYON CROSS-SECTION

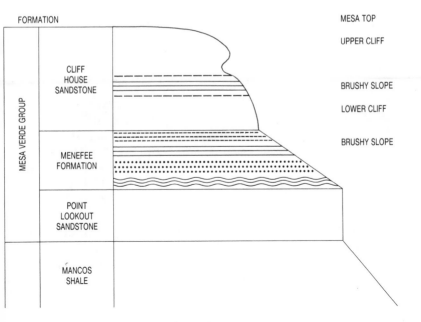

FORMATION

MESA VERDE GROUP

CLIFF HOUSE SANDSTONE

MENEFEE FORMATION

POINT LOOKOUT SANDSTONE

MANCOS SHALE

MESA TOP

UPPER CLIFF

BRUSHY SLOPE

LOWER CLIFF

BRUSHY SLOPE

By the beginning of the Tertiary period of the Cenozoic era, the seas had retreated for the final time. This was around sixty million years ago. Ever so slowly then, the geologic picture began to change. The Southwest started to rise higher, at the same time warping into low domes or depressions. The uplift of the San Juan, La Plata, and Sleeping Ute mountains occurred at this time. Most of these are laccoliths, or intrusive dome mountains, formed by magma thrusting upward but not breaking through the earth's surface. Through the following thousands upon thousands of years crustal movement of the earth continued, and much material was eroded away, only to be redeposited elsewhere.

About a million years ago, the Mesa Verde took on its present flat tableland shape, with a slight downtilt toward the south, a result of the La Plata uplift. Water from rain and melting snow, which probably fell in heavier amounts then than now, gathered in streams that flowed toward the Mancos River which, as the mesa rose, had cut a path south and west through the uplands. The areas of run-off gradually deepened until the southward flowing channels became the deep canyons seen today. The finger-like projections of plateau were left in between. South and east of the Mancos, in that portion of the mesa cut off by the river, the canyons formed in a generally east-west direction. This was the period of time when the overhang formation and the erosion of natural water tanks, or "potholes" occurred. These were both so important to the prehistoric inhabitants of the area, the former for shelter, the latter as a collector, and therefore a source, of water.

Of course the geologic story of the Mesa Verde region is not completed. Erosion of the plateau and its numerous canyons continues. The process of arroyo-cutting is evident along the river, as the water of the Mancos and its tributaries cuts channels ever wider and deeper. In geology, nothing is static. The earth's surface is either eroding or relocating eroded deposits, and it may be rising, falling, or tilting as well.

MANCOS RIVER EROSION
The Mancos River is constantly in the process of cutting away at the bank, ever widening the channel. Eroded material is carried away, to be redeposited elsewhere.

ALCOVES

The alcoves utilized by the Ancient Ones are formed when ground water seeps through porous sandstone. When the downward travel is impeded by a harder layer of rock, usually a shale, the water flows laterally. Where the water emerges from precipitous canyon walls in the form of springs, it erodes the soft sandstone, to leave an overhang of rock above. The entire process is aided by freezing and thawing during seasonal temperature changes. Ice acts as a wedge, resulting in cracks in the rock which eventually slough off in chunks or slabs. Alcoves of all sizes result, usually with sloping rubble-filled talus floors, which often necessitated much labor on the part of the Anasazi to make them habitable.

South and southwest facing caves were favored as construction sites, for the lower winter sun warmed the masonry walls of the dwellings. This heat passed through to other rooms and occasionally to the cliff itself. Less fuel was thus needed. In the summer, the sun was directly overhead and only the front walls of the dwellings felt heat from the sun's rays, while the rest of the village remained cool and comfortable.

CLIMATE AND WEATHER

The Ute Mountain Tribal Park is classified as a semi-arid region, a transitional middle latitude zone that falls somewhere between true desert and a more humid climate. Naturally though, differences in climatic conditions are found throughout the park, in response to elevation and topography. The climate of the lower region along the river differs somewhat from that of the mesa tops, which may be one thousand or more feet higher.

The annual precipitation in nearby Mesa Verde National Park was found to average eighteen inches, with about half of that amount falling as snow. Although it has not been studied as carefully for the Tribal Park, the average, at least nearer to and south of the river, seems to be considerably less.

The critical factor for the growth of plant life is not so much the amount of precipitation, however, but the seasonal distribution. There are usually two peak periods of moisture in the Mesa Verde, one in winter and early spring, and the other in late summer and early autumn. Heavy snowfall between January and March determines the growth of vegetation during late spring and early summer. This was important to the prehistoric human population of the area because they practiced dry-farming techniques. The Anasazi planted their seeds relatively deep, where the winter-deposited moisture would be retained for some time. This nourished the young plants and allowed them to be well-established before the drying heat of summer arrived.

Winter precipitation also provides the water for the "seeps" found in the area, which generally come to life in late spring. The second period of precipitation comes in the form of irregular, often violent, thunderstorms. These begin in mid- to late-summer and can last into early autumn.

Precipitation is the most limiting factor of any ecosystem. It certainly influenced the Anasazi. The Johnson Canyon area appears to receive less moisture than the higher regions of the Mesa Verde proper, and this likely contributed to the earlier abandonment of that region by the Ancient Ones. Tree-ring data shows that yearly moisture totals had significantly lowered even before the long severe drought in the late 1200's.

Weather and temperature vary greatly from winter to summer. During the winter, between periods of snowfall, most days are clear and cool, some relatively warm, especially in Mancos Canyon. In general, winter nights are cold. As is common in semi-arid zones, winter temperatures vary more than those at other times of the year. Spring and fall are pleasant, with normally warm days and cool nights. In summer, it can get quite warm, with daytime temperatures often into the high 90's, or above, especially in canyon bottoms. Nights are generally cool and comfortable.

June is usually the driest month and July the hottest. When the summer storms begin, the heat-- at least near the end of the day--is greatly alleviated. These days of late summer usually begin with cloudless skies but, around noon, the extreme air turbulence has caused cumulus clouds to develop. Precipitation from these storms is most often localized and of short duration. Although heavy amounts of rain occasionally fall during these summer showers, much of the moisture is lost in run-off and provides little benefit for the vegetation.

WATER

Water, what a precious commodity, especially in the high desert, in a semi-arid region. How all-important it must have been to the Ancient Ones. The Anasazi reservoir and irrigation system seen at Far View in the National Park is unusual for this area. For the average Anasazi, it was necessary to plant fields behind catch dams, on small terraces where water from natural run-off would nourish the crops. For everyday use, for drinking, cooking, and bathing, the prehistoric peoples had to rely on other sources.

MORNING SUN ON THE MANCOS
Of all nature's gifts, water was most precious to the Anasazi; it meant survival for them and their crops. A perennial stream, even the Mancos River is unreliable.

The Mancos River is the only permanent source
of water in the area, yet even it can experience
periods of no flow, especially around July.
Although the river has its headwaters in the high
La Plata Mountains, it is the summer and fall
storms that supply the most substantial amount of
annual run-off. Today's river has a controlled
flow, since there is some water allocated for
agricultural use upsteam from the Tribal Park.
During the time of the Anasazi, the river was
undoubtedly a better source of water than it is
now.   Because most of the pueblo ruins of the
Mancos Canyon post-date the cliff dwellings of
Lion Canyon, it is suggested that perhaps the
inhabitants of those alcove villages, after
abandoning their homes, moved closer to the more
reliable river when water in their area became
scarce.

Springs, or "seeps," are a second valuable
source of water.   Almost always located at the
bases of cliffs, many are found at the back of
alcoves, behind Anasazi dwellings.   Undoubtedly,
those caves with their own "running water" were
favored as building sites over those without such
an amenity.   The amount of annual precipitation
greatly influences these springs, of course.   In
drought years, only a scant few might be
permanent. Most would dry up. Even in years of
average to above average precipitation, many
springs are only seasonal. But while they do
flow, they are a good water source.   Sandstone
acts as an aquifer, while the lower shale layers
serve to impede downward flow of water, causing
it to run laterally. It then seeps from the
sandstone at points along the talus slopes of
canyons, clean and cool. The Ancient Ones often
built collecting pools around these seeps, the
remains of which can sometimes still be found.

The third source of water for the Anasazi--
and for the wild life both then and now--is the

standing water found in natural tanks, or "potholes." To be expected, these depend on precipitation. Utilization of the water from these tanks would mostly be reserved for the late summer months, when thunderstorms refill them periodically. The Ancient Ones would have collected the water soon after a storm and stored it in large water jars, called "ollas," for water left in natural tanks does not long remain potable; it soon harbors many forms of life: plant, animal, and bacterial. Also, if the pool is shallow, the water will soon evaporate.

OLLA, or water jar

Used by the Ancient Ones to store water, large ollas were transported to the caves balanced on the heads of Anasazi women. A ring of juniper bast, tied with yucca fibre cord, was often worn on the head to help steady the heavy vessel.

THE STORM
A Second Personal Experience Essay

Over the south rim of the Mancos River Canyon
the sky begins to darken. The "Cloud People" that
dotted the azure blue heavens so innocently all
afternoon have gathered in thick clusters and now
commence to shed their cloaks of white for those
of deep purple-black. Ominous in appearance, they
are an unmistakable portent. A storm is brewing
off to the southwest. In the depths of the canyon
its approach was relatively unnoticed, though
certainly not unexpected, for this is late summer,
the season that brings to the Four Corners region
what the Hopi call the "male" rains--fierce,
strong, sudden.

Thunder rumbles in the distance, the sound
soft, muted. Lightning spears to the earth but it
too is still far away and I cannot witness where
it strikes the mesa. The gentle evening breeze
begins to quicken. It can be heard moving up the
canyon, increasing speed. Suddenly it rounds a
bend in the river gorge. With freight train noise
and velocity, the wind whips into a frenzied fury,
gathering particles of fine sand to lift into
spirals, to send crazily dancing ahead of the
gusts.

Standing on the edge of an unexcavated great
kiva, the wind buffets me as it rushes past,
catching up dry loose grasses, bending the scrub
brush low, frantically twisting the branches of
the tall cottonwoods that grow beside the river.
The dark thunderheads are almost above me now,
moving quickly over the rim to fill the canyon,
the noise they emit magnified as the storm center

84

nears, the interval between light flashes and sound ever shorter.

Time to head for shelter, I decide, but my son, John, has not yet returned. He is off exploring the plateau above me, mapping out the plan of additional large ceremonial structures located there. Growing anxious, I leave the pile of pottery sherds I had gathered to examine and photograph, and move off to scan first the threatening sky, then the mesa above. I soon distinguish the form of my son as he makes a hurried descent of the steep, rocky hillside, following a pathway that undoubtedly dates to the time of the Anasazi. He returns; we have little to say to each other. The same thought is in both our minds. At a brisk walk we start the mile trek back to camp.

STORM
Storm clouds gather over the south rim of Mancos Canyon. The lower unexcavated Great Kiva at Kiva Point lies in the foreground.

Great bean-sized drops of water begin to fall, to spatter on dusty road and tingle on skin bared for the August heat. This is to be no light drizzle, it quickly becomes apparent, and I am not dressed for a storm. An oversight on my part, for I am certainly familiar with the vagaries of Southwest weather. But this was to be a pleasant evening stroll, after a hard day of rigorous hiking and strenuous climbing in the hot summer sunshine, exploring Soda and Cliff Canyons. Just an easy after-dinner walk to look over Kiva Point, an area rare for the Mesa Verde.

In the National Park, Morfield Great Kiva was partially excavated, then filled in again. Similar partial excavation was carried out on another oversized round chamber on the mesa top near Johnson Canyon. But this cluster of probable Great Kivas near the Mancos River is quite possibly the only one of its kind. Because these kivas are several miles distant from high density population centers, their location must have had definite ceremonial significance. John and I had planned to take our time, to study, to speculate on what might lay beneath the tons of soil and rubble that have filled in the sunken structures so long abandoned. And although the clouding up of an afternoon is common, not often does it result in the dropping of much moisture.

Usually.

The rain comes harder, increased to a real torrent. My son has come prepared, at least. He stops, takes a rain jacket from his day pack and insists that I wear it. Claps of thunder ever nearer echo menacingly up and down the canyon, forcing us to hasten our pace. At a jog trot, we continue on.

The two of us are alone in the canyon. No one else is staying at the small Ute Tribal Park campground by the river, and it has been years since any of the Mountain Utes called the canyon home. Even our guides for the day have long since returned to the comfort of their homes in Towaoc. "We're city Indians," Park Director, Arthur Cuthair, had teased earlier in the day. They don't stay out in the "wilderness" unless taking visitors on backpacking trips, he explained.

But are we truly alone? I wonder. There is such a sense of "aliveness" to the canyon, the river, the majestic sandstone cliffs that surround us. There is more than just electricity in the turbulent air, an almost tangible presence. Perhaps the spirits of the Ancient Ones have come out to greet the storm, to offer prayerful thanksgiving for its appearance. How welcome would have been this rain in the days of the prolonged droughts of the twelfth and thirteenth centuries, those cursed times when the gods failed to impregnate the Cloud People with precious moisture and allow them to birth the life-sustaining element so necessary to the survival of the Anasazi. Yes, both John and I agree, the spirits are felt everywhere, in the relentless pelting rain, the clashing thunder, the shriek of tree-lashing wind. More lighting, more thunder, a harder fall of rain follows, and our pace is again quickened.

Despite our haste, we thoroughly enjoy the experience, liking the feel of the hard drops of water that stream down faces upturned to the angry gray sky, rain that plasters hair to heads, that soaks clothing, shoes. For it cannot dampen our enthusiasm. There is nothing to equal a desert storm, its quickness, its fury, its raw power.

Camp is reached while the storm is at its height. Inside our camper, which vibrates with each roar of thunder, we change into dry clothing, then sit to watch the tempest raging outside. It does not last long. Summer showers rarely do. The black clouds move on up the canyon and roll over the rim to the northeast. For awhile afterwards, rivulets of water pour down our back window. They soon decrease to steady plopping drops, until these too diminish entirely. Outside, dark-foliaged juniper, silver-tinged sagebrush, and red-berried squawbush shimmer as the sky lightens, the sun briefly returning, its lowering rays chasing the retreating storm. No longer wishing to remain indoors, we go out where the air smells clean, fresh, exhilarating. The sky is again clear. The life-giving rain is gone for another day, another week, perhaps longer. The ground has gratefully soaked up the moisture, been renewed.

As is typical in the high desert of the Southwest, within the hour there is little evidence of the storm's passing.

MAIN RUINS TOUR

The tour to the main ruins of Lion Canyon begins at the Ute Mountain Pottery Factory. In your own vehicle, you follow your guide(s) south on highway 666, turning east after about eight miles toward Jackson Butte, named in honor of William H. Jackson. A monolith detached from the west rim of Mesa Verde, it is also called Chimney Rock. Near the base of this distinctive landmark, the tour group stops at the Ute Tribal Park Visitor Center, a recently constructed building fashioned in the manner of an ancient pueblo.

VISITOR CENTER
Constructed by Ute Mountain youth, this modern rendition of an ancient pueblo was built to house the park visitor center and museum.

Once inside the visitor center, a descent is made via ladder to a tunnel which takes you into a kiva. There, explanations about the features and use of a ceremonial chamber are given. This stone and wood structure was built by members of the Ute Summer Youth Program. Wherever possible, work on the park is done by the Utes themselves, thereby providing needed employment opportunities.

Back in your vehicle, you are soon traveling into Mancos Canyon and approaching the river. The second stop on the tour is usually at an unexcavated pueblo ruin, called Red Pottery Site. Many mounds such as this are found throughout the canyon and on the surrounding mesa tops. This particular site was a small village, which probably housed only a few extended family or clan groupings. In addition to the living and storage rooms, there are two indentations that indicate kivas, and rubble from a probable tower. Although numerous pieces of red pottery can be seen scattered at the site--hence the name--it is generally believed that most red ware in the Mesa Verde was a trade item and, because of the scarcity of the necessary clay, not often locally produced. Most of the scattered surface potsherds are from black-on-white vessels of several different design periods, or are from plain gray or gray corrugated cook ware.

After you leave Red Pottery Site and the canyon begins to narrow, watch for Tower Ruin on your right, across the river. Your guide may or may not stop to point this out, depending on time, the number in your group, or other factors. Towers generally date from late Developmental Pueblo or Classic Pueblo times. Most are round, single or double-walled, but some are D-shaped or rectangular. Quite often a tower was connected to a kiva. Their exact purpose is unknown; archaeologists can only speculate. Towers here in the canyon were described in great detail in the

Hayden Government Survey reports of 1874 through 1876. From these descriptions, it is readily apparent that the towers have deteriorated considerably during the last century. If you miss seeing this tower, the rubble of another one can be viewed when the group stops at Kiva Point, farther along on the tour.

On your left as you continue up the canyon you might spot occasional rock art tucked beneath sandstone overhangs. The red paint and style of much of this art work indicates that most are Ute paintings, and not Anasazi. Except for the petroglyph panels at Kiva Point, little significant Anasazi art work has been found in the region.

Farther along on your right can be seen a rock formation called Train Rock, named for its resemblance to a steam engine and cars. A small Anasazi ruin is perched atop this rock, although little remains of the structure. Richard Wetherill was an early visitor here, for he inscribed a poem in the rock by the ruin.

Watch the cliff face all along the Mancos River Canyon; you might catch sight of ruins. Nearly all the ones in this area are small. Although some might have provided temporary housing for a few individuals, most were likely used for storage. Corn was the crop generally kept in these "granaries." It was often stored for months, occasionally longer, with the doorways sealed until the produce was needed.

Your next stop on the tour will be at the site where once stood the "hogan," or home of Chief Jack House, the last chief of the Ute Mountain Utes. Your guide will give a brief description of him and his importance to the Tribal Park. Prime examples of Ute pictographs (paintings) can also be seen in the rocks here, as well as one set of probable Anasazi negative-image "hand prints." To accomplish the later symbol, the hand was placed against the rock, paint was blown through a hollow reed around the hand, then the hand was removed. The purpose of these hand prints, found all over the four-corners region, is uncertain. As with all rock art, many interpretations have been hypothesized, none proven conclusively.

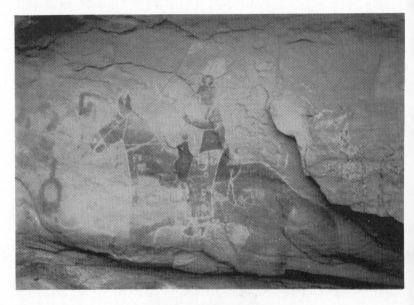

UTE PICTOGRAPH
This painting of a cowboy and horse is typical of Ute art work in the canyon. Big and bold in design, the Utes favored the use of red paint.

A site of probable Anasazi cannibalism lies farther on, although it is doubtful your guide will stop here, as the road now covers the area where the find was made. When salvage archaeology was done for the road bed, the workers came upon a room where the bones of about thirty-five people were found. These bones had been pried apart with a stick in order to get at the marrow. Thereafter, they were stacked neatly in a corner of the room. Cannibalism was apparently quite rare among the Ancient Ones. Conditions resulting from the drought may have forced its occurrence. Also found here was the mummy of a baby. This was left in place. Anywhere that a road is proposed, salvage work must be carried out in order to save information otherwise lost. Some places that you travel may pass directly over a former Anasazi home.

On most tours your guide will stop to show visitors the "footprint" rock. This is a baffling geologic oddity. The sandstone boulder seems to show the footprints of a person who stood here in the mud some hundreds of thousands of years ago, when the area was on the shoreline of an ancient sea. Yet man was not supposed to reside on this continent at that time. It may be left for future generations to unravel the mystery of these strange footprints.

Kiva Point is an area of major archaeological importance, and is the next stop on your tour. This point of land lies at the southern end of Chapin Mesa, which continues northward into Mesa Verde National Park. The numerous unexcavated ruins in this area cover a time period from about A.D. 800 to A.D. 1250, although there is speculation that some sites may cover earlier pithouse remains.

Many sites dot both the lower and upper levels of Kiva Point. On the lower level can be seen the depression of a Great Kiva, with perhaps as many as three rows of associated rooms on at least two sides. A double-walled tower and adjoining kiva are nearby, and several other habitation sites. Part way up the cliff and to the right can be seen a cliff dwelling, estimated to have had from eight to fifteen rooms. Several rock art panels with many petroglyphs (drawings pecked into stone) lie just below these ruins.

ANASAZI PETROGLYPHS
A petroglyph panel at Kiva Point. Nearly all the symbols pecked in this rock were done by the Anasazi. Their exact meaning is open to speculation.

On the upper level of Kiva Point is found the Great Kiva complex. Tour groups normally do not have time to visit this area, but mention will be made of what is to be found on that higher level. There are three large depressions--the biggest measuring sixty-two feet across--with a few rows of rooms possibly separating the larger depression from the other two. The complex contains the rubble of a two-story rectangular room block with two small associated kivas. A short distance to the north and nearer to the highest level of Chapin Mesa is another unexcavated pueblo village, this one with perhaps thirty to forty rooms and two kivas. The population of the immediate area offers no apparent justification for such a concentration of Great Kivas. That the complex held important ceremonial significance for the Anasazi cannot be questioned. For what reason is unknown. Perhaps future excavation will at least partially answer questions about this special area.

About a mile beyond Kiva Point, shortly before you reach the Johnson Canyon turnoff, is the entrance to the Ute Mountain Tribal Park campground. Several campsites lie hidden among the juniper and sage near the river, each with well-constructed firepit and table. Pit toilets are nearby and water is usually made available during the summer, but there are no hookups for recreational vehicles. The seclusion and peacefulness of the canyon, along with its rugged scenic beauty, makes it a pleasant place to stay if semi-primitive conditions are not a deterrent. Remember, you must obtain a permit from the Utes in order to do so.

The Johnson Canyon road takes you quickly, via several switchbacks, up and out of Mancos Canyon to the mesa tops southeast of the river. Visible occasionally in the first few miles of travel is the deep defile of Johnson Canyon off to your left. While some of the country you now pass through is forested, much of the area is grass or sagebrush. A large part of the plateau here was "chained" in the near past, a method of clearing the land to encourage grass growth for the running of cattle. The broad vistas from this open country are wondrous. North is the towering La Plata range, west is Sleeping Ute Mountain, and to the south can be seen the erosion-exposed volcanic skeleton of Shiprock, New Mexico.

After several miles and a few changes in direction, you will arrive near the confluence of Lion and Johnson Canyons, where the vehicles are parked for a short walk to the mesa rim. From the confluence point, locally called "Lover's Leap," you look across the canyon to the cliff dwelling named Eagle's Nest, a ruin quite unusual in setting and construction. Although not all are visible from any one place on the rim, to the right of Eagle's Nest is Morris 5, then Lion House, and around the corner, tucked back out of sight, is Tree House. These are the four villages you will soon visit. Also, a walk along the canyon rim to the east from the parking area will bring you to the head of a short side canyon where Fortified House can be seen in the cliff below. This is the ruin in which the Wetherills and Charles Mason made major finds. (See chapter on History of Archaeological Discovery)

Returning to your vehicle, the tour group backtracks to a cutoff that heads Lion Canyon, to approach the Main Ruins area from the northeast. After your travel through still more chained fields and one section burned by a forest fire, you will find yourself back in a thick pinyon-juniper forest. At the parking area where the Main Ruins tour begins, there is a picnic table and pit toilet for visitor convenience. Most groups eat lunch here before beginning the hike to the cliff dwellings. REMEMBER: You must provide your own lunch for this day long outing.

A short walk to the north rim of Lion Canyon brings you to the start of the Main Ruins trail. Almost immediately it becomes necessary to descend a series of ladders to reach the ruins level. Made from native materials, these pole ladders are sturdy, well-braced, and not dangerous if reasonable care is taken. Small children, however, might have difficulty with the wide-spaced rungs and need assistance. A few steps carved in or built of stone also help deliver the tourist to the base of the cliff, where the first dwelling visited is Tree House.

Named for the tall stand of douglas fir that thrives in this moist, shaded area, Tree House has twenty-seven living and storage rooms and three kivas. Tree-rings date the structure to around A.D. 1200. A few of the walls still have the original plaster on their outer face, but the paint that you see on the inside of the main kiva has been reconstructed. Although you are welcome to explore most of the village, please stay out of the roped off areas. They have not been stabilized and are extra delicate.

FRAMED DOORWAY

This door in Tree House was framed with mortar on the inside. A sandstone slab lies just below, a perfect fit. The room could only be closed from the outside in this manner.

At the east end of Tree House is a three-story tower and adjacent upper rooms. This tower has one original floor/ceiling still intact. The interior burned at one time, a frequent occurrence during Anasazi occupation, whenever fires were built inside rooms.

Gustaf Nordenskiold visited the village and collected surface artifacts. Both Al and John Wetherill carved their names on a boulder that the Anasazi used to sharpen their axe heads. The inscription dates differ, indicating that the brothers explored the dwelling more than once, or remained several days. Earl Morris later excavated part of this ruin, also, as did the University of Colorado to prepare the park for visitation.

The second cliff village visited is Lion House, the largest on the tour. This fine alcove town has approximately forty-six rooms and six (or possibly seven) kivas. In 1974, twelve of the rooms and four of the ceremonial chambers were excavated by the University of Colorado archaeological team. Another unexcavated kiva, oddly shaped, has a wattle and daub (stick and mud) deflector, rare for the time in which it was supposedly built.

This village, however, experienced two different periods of construction, as did most others in the canyon. From tree-ring core samples, archaeologists have determined that building occurred between the A.D. 1130's and 1150. A break in occupation of the alcove followed, which corresponds to a drought period in the region. The second construction phase began about A.D. 1195 and lasted until the early 1240's. Almost all the architecture that remains dates to this latter time period, but much of the material incorporated obviously came from dismantled earlier habitations.

LION HOUSE

The largest village visited on the Main Ruins tour of Ute Mountain Tribal Park, many exciting finds were made during excavation of this cliff dwelling.

CRAFT SPECIALIZATION

When archaeologists excavated part of Lion House, fifty pairs of woven yucca sandals were found in one area. This is only a medium-sized village. Most likely the footwear was made by one man, the village sandalmaker, who traded his shoes all over the region for other goods needed by him and his family. The specialization of crafts was undoubtedly a common practice, and the barter system frequently employed by the Anasazi. Why these sandals were manufactured, then left behind, is unknown. Perhaps it was easier to make others later, than to transport them when the sandalmaker moved.

Between Lion House and the next cliff village, Morris 5, look for a small overhanging rock beside the path, where a few bones and pottery pieces lay scattered on the sand. This is a human burial site. Depending on the size of your group or how far apart you have become on this narrow trail, your guide may or may not point these out. Also, it is not uncommon to see bones in the villages; some are from the former occupants.

BURIAL SITE
These human bones and a few scattered potsherds are all that remain of an Anasazi burial.

All along the path between the four villages you will see excellent examples of the plant life indigenous to the region. Watch for pinyon pine, Mormon tea, broadleaf yucca, squawbush--and poison ivy. The latter is prevalent in the wet, shady areas at the cliff base, and the path passes quite near the noxious plant in several places.

Morris 5, named because that was the number assigned to the ruin by Earl Morris, contains seventeen living and storage rooms and two kivas, one of which was excavated in 1974. Take note of the original roof beams that are still in place. Also notice the difference between the two kivas. See how much dirt and rubble fills the still untouched kiva. Take time to examine the artifacts both here and in the other ruins. Much can be learned about the vanished people from the cultural remains they left behind. But don't forget--make certain these artifacts are left behind when YOU leave, also.

This ruin, Morris 5, dates from the early 1200's. Again there is indication of earlier occupation, evidenced by the re-use of one kiva beam that was cut sometime during the 1140's. Notice also the stone work on the upper, inaccessible level of the ruin. No mortar was used there, the rocks were merely stacked. That was a common practice during dry years when water was precious. In any case, this higher area was probably used only for storage.

Eagle's Nest is the last cliff dwelling on the tour. It is tucked beneath a yawning overhang, built on an almost unreachable ledge which protrudes from the cliff wall. Although there is evidence that the original inhabitants used a single long tree trunk as ladder to gain access from below, the only way now to enter and exit the village is by using the thirty foot ladder constructed by the Utes for that purpose-- or by rappelling from the rim above. One person at a time is the best method to employ on the ladder. Be extra careful from then on, too, for the path is "edgy" and low enough in one place that most everyone must duck the head. Even if you decide not to enter the village, much can be viewed from below, and other rooms can also be visited there.

LADDER

Access to the village of Eagle's Nest is via this thirty foot ladder, then along a narrow, low-roofed ledge.

Eagle's Nest, a small village, contains thirteen rooms and one kiva. It was probably inhabited by only one extended family. There are also five more rooms at the base of the cliff, their purpose uncertain.

The one ceremonial chamber here in Eagle's Nest is a fine example of a plastered, painted kiva. From ten to twelve layers of white clay were applied to the inner wall. Around the circumference, the lower half was painted red-brown. A series of three triangles is repeated at intervals above this middle line, with small dots visible in between. In historic times, this exceptional kiva also had an intact roof. When archaeologist Morris excavated the village in 1913, he desired to photograph the painted interior and, having no flash for his camera, removed the roof. Off to the side you can see where he deposited the roofing materials. If left alone, this kiva would have been among a select few ever found in a cliff dwelling with the original roof in place.

EAGLE'S NEST
The timbers protruding from the wall originally served as the framework for a balcony that probably ran the length of the village. The Anasazi apparently had little fear of heights.

Look out over the edge at the front of the village. (Be very careful, please!) The sticks seen protruding from the masonry walls indicate that at one time a balcony ran across the front of the dwellings. This facilitated getting from one room to another without disturbing neighbors. Imagine yourself on that narrow walkway, high above the canyon depths. It would not have been good to be afraid of heights if you were an Anasazi.

Also of interest in Eagle's Nest is a wall, about a foot high, that runs laterally along the back of the cave. It is speculated that this might have been some form of a "central heating" system. It appears too small to have been a passageway, nor is it a likely area for storage. However, a fire built at one end might have sent sufficient warm air flowing through the tunnel to heat the rooms. Ingenious, if true.

LEAVING EAGLE'S NEST
Visitors cross the sloping rock ledge as they return to the ladder and a careful descent to the cliff base. The room pictured is separate from the main village.

This is the end of the tour. From here you retrace your path back to the car-park area. There, you will be asked to sign a guest register and give your impression of what you have seen. You may also pay for the tour at this time, if you have not already done so. Gratuities are appreciated if you feel that your experience was worth more than the regular fee.

As you say good-by to your guides and drive from Ute Mountain Tribal Park, take note of all you see around you. Imagine living in the time of the Ancient Ones, coping with the harsh environment, with only the natural resources available to you. You would soon learn to be one with nature, a part of the land...or you would not long survive.

UNEXCAVATED POT
This corrugated cook pot, and one other similar, still rest in the floor-fill of an unexcavated kiva.

HIKING AND BACKPACKING

Most of the 125,000 acres of Ute Mountain Tribal Park is wild and untamed, far removed from all vestiges of civilization, untenanted by any save coyote and rabbit, lizard and hawk. Few roads penetrate this land of cliff-bordered canyons and high-jutting mesas. Those trails that do enter the region give access to a primitive wonderland, where each canyon may hold a new surprise: A small herd of wild horses, a golden eagle soaring overhead, such mystery and majesty in his stare, or an alcove containing an almost invisible cliff dwelling few have ever entered. It is a remote area of secluded Anasazi ruins, mysterious, almost forbidding in appearance, ruins that often evoke in the visitor a deep feeling of awe, wonder, an emotion rare and perhaps unexpected. All of this makes the park a perfect place for hiking trips of one to several days. With the Utes as gracious hosts and well-informed guides, the opportunities for wilderness exploration are almost limitless.

The favorite area for backpacking is the region that lies between the west rim of the Mesa Verde and the boundary of the National Park, and from the northern rim to the plateau edge that borders the Mancos River. Vehicle access to this area is possible in a few places, mainly in Navajo and Ute Canyons. Transportation is usually provided for visitors on these special trips, as four-wheel drive is sometimes required on the rough, sandy trails. Guides can take you on various interesting day hikes from these access points, provided you have made prior arrangements. But to traverse this rugged land from east to west

BACKPACKERS PREPARING
Getting ready for a two night, cross country trip, these backpackers check their equipment, make final adjustments.

or north to south (or in reverse) a minimum stay of two or more days is required.

A typical two night backpacking trip begins at Park Headquarters in Towaoc. Directions to the office will be given when your trip arrangements are made. Your personal vehicle is left in town, safe in a locked, fenced yard. You and your group will be driven to the canyon of the Mancos, eventually turning north into Navajo Canyon, then up one of its tributaries, Rock Canyon. This is where your party, your guides, and all the equipment will be left. REMEMBER: You must bring everything you need, including food and water. On foot, you work your way north and west across the Mesa Verde, through sometimes trackless virgin forest, making your way around (or in and out of) seven-hundred-foot-deep canyons, climb to hidden, often virtually inaccessible cliff dwellings, until the west rim is reached. After a steep descent is made, your backpacking party will be met and transported back to town.

Another area favored for exploration, although not as often visited, is located south of the river, in the region of Grass Canyon. An old jeep trail is followed into the canyon, where several dozen Anasazi dwellings dot the cliffs along its twisting length. The terrain is somewhat different here, especially near the mouth of the canyon where the elevation is lower. This is a good place to study the geologic layer known as the Menefee formation, with its interesting coal deposits. Greesewood Canyon, the largest tributary of Grass Canyon, is another good hiking prospect, and is sometimes included on backpacking trips in this part of the park.

The guides for these excursions into the back country are extremely knowledgeable. They know where to locate the most reliable sources of water, the best camping sites, or the most interesting ruins to visit. Even if you request to explore an area new to your guides (and this can happen, with the park so large) they unerringly seem to find the best route across country, the very same toe-and-hand-hold approach used by the Anasazi to reach a certain cliff dwelling, or the way to a hidden spring. This is an ability inherent in their nature, perhaps. It is this understanding, this feel for and love of the land, along with the wit and enthusiasm of Arthur Cuthair and his staff, that makes any trip, be it for a day or a week, a worthwhile and unforgettable outdoor experience.

In planning any hiking trip, however, certain factors must be considered, and cannot be stressed enough. This is rough, arid country, with frequently high daytime summer temperatures. Heat can cause problems for those not accustomed. Always wear a hat and carry sufficient water. Salt tablets are also helpful. The altitude, of from 5,000 to 7,000 feet, although not truly high, might be a problem for those from lower elevations. A slower walking pace than usual might have to be adopted. Canyon walls are sheer and drop-offs sudden, and slopes are steep and often consist of loose talus. Extreme care must be exercised at all times. It is best to be in good physical condition and have proper equipment and foot gear. These warnings are not meant to be discouraging, but are given in order that you can plan accordingly. It is also reassuring to know that radio contact is always maintained between the guides and Towaoc, in the event of an emergency.

DAY HIKING
This hike in lower Soda Canyon, later continuing into Cliff Canyon, is typical of the many options available for day hikes in Ute Tribal Park. Director, Arthur Cuthair, leads the way.

There are many other sections of the vast Ute Mountain Tribal Park which can be visited, beyond those mentioned herein, as well as numerous variations of the examples given. It is best to talk to the Park Director for specific information. With Mr. Cuthair, you can discuss your interests, what you wish to see and do, and your limitations, if any. Suggestions will be made. From these you can decide where you want to go. The area is primitive, to explore it properly may be physically challenging, but there is one guarantee: If it is the unusual you are seeking, you will not be disappointed.

LION HOUSE METATES

BIBLIOGRAPHY

Ambler, J. Richard, THE ANASAZI, PREHISTORIC PEOPLE OF THE FOUR CORNERS REGION, Flagstaff, AZ, Museum of Northern Arizona 1977

Barnes, F. A. and Michaelene Pendleton, CANYON COUNTRY PREHISTORIC INDIANS, Salt Lake City, UT, Wasatch Publications, 1979

Breternitz, David A., CULTURAL RESOURCE INVENTORY OF THE KIVA POINT LOCALITY, UTE MOUNTAIN UTE HOMELAND, Boulder, CO, University of Colorado archaeological report, 1977

Cassells, E. Steve, THE ARCHAEOLOGY OF COLORADO, Boulder, CO, Johnson Publishing Co., 1983

Elmore, Francis H., SHRUBS AND TREES OF THE SOUTHWEST UPLANDS, Globe, AZ, Southwest Parks and Monuments Association, Inc. 1976

Erdman, James A., Charles L. Douglas, and John W. Marr, ENVIRONMENT OF MESA VERDE, COLORADO, Washington, D.C., National Park Service, 1969

Ferguson, William M., and Arthur H. Rohn, ANASAZI RUINS OF THE SOUTHWEST IN COLOR, Albuquerque, N M, University of New Mexico Press, 1987

Fletcher, Maurine S., THE WETHERILLS OF THE MESA VERDE, AUTOBIOGRAPHY OF BENJAMIN ALFRED WETHERILL, Cranbury, N J, Associated University Presses, Inc., 1977

Hughes, J. Donald, AMERICAN INDIANS OF COLORADO, Boulder, CO, Pruett Publishing Co., reprinted from University of Denver, Department of History, 1977

Jackson, William H. and William M. Holmes, MESA VERDE AND THE FOUR CORNERS, Ouray, CO, Bear Creek Publishing Co., reprint from the Hayden Survey, 1981

Kelly, George W., USEFUL PLANTS OF THE 4-CORNERS STATES, Cortez, CO, Rocky Mountain Horticultural Publishing Co., 1980

Lister, Florence C. and Robert H. Lister, EARL MORRIS AND SOUTHWESTERN ARCHAEOLOGY, Albuquerque, N M, University of New Mexico Press, 1968

Marsh, Charles S., PEOPLE OF THE SHINING MOUNTAINS, Boulder, CO, Pruett Publishing Co., 1982

McNitt, Frank, RICHARD WETHERILL: ANASAZI, Albuquerque, N M, University of New Mexico Press, 1957, revised in 1966

Nickens, Paul R., PUEBLO III COMMUNITIES IN TRANSITION: ENVIRONMENT AND ADAPTATION IN JOHNSON CANYON, Boulder, CO, Colorado Archaeological Society in cooperation with the University of Colorado, 1981

Nordenskiold, Gustaf, THE CLIFF DWELLERS OF THE MESA VERDE, Glorieta, New Mexico, The Rio Grande Press, Inc., 1893, reprinted 1980

Pettit, Jan, UTES, THE MOUNTAIN PEOPLE, Colorado Springs, CO, Century One Press, 1982

PICTOGRAPH TRAIL GUIDE, Mesa Verde Museum Association, Inc.

Reed, Verner Z., THE SOUTHERN UTE INDIANS OF EARLY COLORADO, Edgemont, CO, Outbooks, 1980, reprinted from 1893

Rigby, J. Kieth, SOUTHERN COLORADO PLATEAU FIELD GUIDE, Dubuque, IA, Kendall/Hunt Publishing Co., 1977

Simrak, David T., THE GEOLOGIC STORY OF MESA VERDE COUNTRY, Cortez, CO. David T. Simrak, 1983

Watson, Don, INDIANS OF THE MESA VERDE, Mesa Verde National Park, CO, Mesa Verde Museum Association, Inc. 1953

Wenger, Gilbert R., THE STORY OF MESA VERDE NATIONAL PARK, Mesa Verde Museum Association, Inc., 1980

Wenger, Stephen R., FLOWERS OF MESA VERDE NATIONAL PARK, Mesa Verde National Park, CO, Mesa Verde Museum Association, Inc. 1976

Back cover:
TREE HOUSE TOWER

NOTES

NOTES

NOTES

NOTES

NOTES

NOTES

NOTES

NOTES

NOTES

NOTES

NOTES